WONDER DOGS

101 German Shepherd Dog Films

WONDER DOGS

101 German Shepherd Dog Films

Jordan Taylor

Reel Dogs Press
Bainbridge Island

Published by:
Reel Dogs Press

An imprint of:
Adoxography Books
P.O. Box 11607
Bainbridge Island, WA 98110

First edition.
12 10 09   5 4 3 2 1
Printed and bound in the USA.

Library of Congress Cataloging-in-Publication Data

Taylor, Jordan,
Wonder dogs: 101 german shepherd dog films
p. cm.
Includes biographical references and index.
ISBN 978-0-9800090-0-2 (alk. paper)
1. Animals in motion pictures. 2. German shepherd dogs. 3. Motion pictures—dogs—history. 4. Motion pictures—United States—
history and criticism. 5. Motion Pictures—international—history
and criticism. I Title: Wonder dogs: 101 german shepherd dog
films II. Jordan Taylor

Front cover: Canczech's Solo, owned by Tony and Katie Nikl,
2009.
Back cover: Peter the Great, circa 1925.

Dedicated to the memory of the first hero of movie German Shepherd trainers: Lee Duncan (1892–1960). Also to the most recent: Karl Lewis Miller (1941–2008).

And to the thousands of German Shepherd Dogs who have ever graced a screen with their beauty and intelligence.

Table of Contents

Wonder Dogs

101 German Shepherd Dog Films

Introduction

For almost one hundred years, German Shepherd Dogs have been starring in movies of every genre, all over the world. Achieving success in more diverse roles than Meryl Streep, and with far less demanding salaries, GSDs have been wowing audiences with feats of bravery, intelligence, and physical skill for nearly as long as the breed has existed. Playing everything from guards to guides, wolves to war heroes, German Shepherds have helped countless human costars solve the crime, right the wrong, track down the bad guy, and save the day.

Beginning in 1921 with a dog named Strongheart, Hollywood studios started seeing German Shepherds, or "police dogs," as an audience draw equal to, or better than, many human celebrities of the time. After Strongheart on the silent screen came Rin-Tin-Tin, Peter the Great, Fearless, Ranger, Dynamite, Thunder, Flash, and many more—usually receiving top billing and titles after their names like "The Wonder Dog," "The Famous Police Dog," "The Dog Marvel," and (for Fearless) "The Greatest of All Dog Actors."

Although the GSD movie-star fad of the 1920s began to die down with the introduction of sound to films, when spoken dialogue became a noticeable advantage to human actors, the breed still saw success in the form of specific, name-recognized dogs through the 1940s. The sons and grandsons of Strongheart, Rin-Tin-Tin, and Flash, as well as new dogs, moved in to take the place of silent stars.

From the end of the 1930s and through the 1940s came a new type of GSD film. Instead of action genres with adult casts, such as western, war, crime, and wilderness, that previous dogs starred in, new GSD movies featured innumerable boy-and-his-dog plots. The dogs still with some name recognition, like Ace and Flame, were in more and more features with children as the target audience. With some exceptions—Chinook, for example, and TV stars J.R. and Rin Tin Tin IV—the German Shepherd had lost its place as a recognizable name draw even on a small scale by the 1950s. Though still a popular breed for the movies, a canine who received top billing had become a thing of the past.

The breed saw somewhat of a revival, film-wise, in the 1970s, when a large number of Euro westerns featuring German Shepherds were made, and the canine horror genre emerged with films like *The Pack* (1977) and the made-for-TV movie *Devil Dog: The Hound of Hell* (1978). GSDs also made a great breed for film families in need of protection, a concept used in *The Hills Have Eyes* (1977) and *Dracula's Dog* (1978), in which the humans need protection from the title dog, a Doberman Pinscher.

By the 1990s, German Shepherds had fallen into roles we are still seeing today, playing central parts in everything from children's made-for-TV and straight-to-DVD movies to major box-office drama and comedy features. Though it has been a very long time since one made top billing over human costars, there are still German Shepherd actors who receive a fair amount of attention: Jerry Lee (played by a dog named Rando) was credited on the lobby cards right next to James Belushi in *K-9* (1989); the GSD stars of long-running Austrian TV show *Kommissar Rex* and movie tie-in *Baby Rex* (1997) have achieved international fame; and Abbey, who played Samantha in *I Am Legend* (2007), received a huge amount of press coverage and appeared alongside Will Smith at the premiere.

This book highlights 101 of the hundreds, or thousands, of German Shepherd Dog films produced since 1921. Some of the films may be lost or extremely difficult to find on DVD—many more are readily available or available through small movie dealers and private collectors selling online.

Where status of a film is given as "limited availability," the film is either available on DVD from small dealers or has never been released on DVD and is only available on used VHS. Where status is given as "rare," the film may be extremely difficult to find in any format and has never commercially been released on either VHS or DVD.

A list of websites where you can purchase most of the films profiled can be found in the back of this book.

Happy viewing!

The Beginning: The 1920s

By the 1920s, dogs had already made their mark on film history. Blair, a Collie, starred in the first dog movie, *Rescued by Rover* (1905). Luke, an American Pit Bull Terrier, costarred in dozens of short films in the 1910s. Jean, "The Vitagraph Dog," also starred in shorts of the 1910s. Teddy, Props, and Brownie were some other early canine stars—though none were German Shepherds. The 1920s launched a new era of dogs in film, one in which a dog could not only star in his or her own short, but could receive top billing in a feature film—a concept pioneered and maintained by German Shepherd Dogs throughout the decade.

The Silent Call (1921)

GSD: Strongheart as *Flash*
Trainer: Laurence Trimble
Director: Laurence Trimble
Costars: John Bowers, Kathryn McGuire
Country: USA
Status: Unknown

Based on the novel *The Cross Pull*, by Hal G. Evarts, *The Silent Call* was one of the first movies to star a German Shepherd—another, *Kazan*, having been released less than two weeks earlier. The dog's name was Etzel von Oeringen, but he went by the call name Strongheart after Jane Murfin and her husband, Laurence Trimble, brought him from Germany to America in 1920. Trimble, who had trained the first name-recognized canine movie star, Jean, began at once re-socializing the aloof military dog to have a more relaxed and friendly disposition so he could start work on the film.

Strongheart plays Flash—in the novel a wolf/coyote/dog cross—whose master, Clark Moran (John Bowers), must leave his rural home and travel to the city. Flash is falsely accused of sheep killing but escapes a death sentence, fleeing to the wilderness. He takes up with a she-wolf, returning to civilization to save a lady in distress, Betty (Kathryn McGuire), catch the bad guys, and reunite with Clark.

Critics were skeptical of Trimble's idea to import a dog for the sole purpose of starring in his own movies, but everything changed when *The Silent Call* grossed $1,000,000 at the box office. Strongheart was an instant star. *The New York Times* said of him in the film, "Strongheart, the police dog . . . is a magnificent creature, an excellent photographic subject, and an interesting performer." He went on to star in four more films, all well received, including the first screen adaptation of Jack London's *White Fang* (1925).

Where the North Begins (1923)

GSD: Rin-Tin-Tin as the dog
Trainer: Lee Duncan
Director: Chester M. Franklin
Costars: Claire Adams, Walter McGrail
Country: USA
Status: Limited availability

When Rin-Tin-Tin landed his first starring role two years after *The Silent Call*, *The New York Times* wrote that, while the new dog was interesting, he "suffers in comparison with Strongheart."

In September 1918, Corporal Lee Duncan of the 135th Aero Squadron rescued a German Shepherd and her newborn litter while serving in France. He kept two (the rest were also adopted), naming them after the French story and good-luck dolls, Nanette (or Nannette) and Rintintin. The following spring, he returned to America with the two pups, but

Nanette died of pneumonia shortly after they arrived. Duncan started showing Rin-Tin-Tin until a judge told him the dog was "clumsy." Prompted by the insult, Duncan began intensive training with his dog that would change both their lives. In 1923, after two minor film roles, Rin-Tin-Tin received his first starring credit with Warner Brothers in *Where the North Begins*.

Rin-Tin-Tin plays a dog raised by wolves who reverts to his domesticated nature when he saves a wounded trapper, Gabriel Dupré (Walter McGrail), from wolves (Siberian Huskies). He also saves Gabriel from the Fox (Charles Stevens), who had been hired by the evil Shad Galloway (Pat Hartigan) to kill Gabriel, and rescues him from freezing, all in one day. He then accompanies Gabriel back to his remote home and fiancée, Felice (Claire Adams). There's still much for the canine hero to do as Rin-Tin-Tin uncovers the bad guys, rescues Felice, and makes an incredible leap into a second-story window of Gabriel's cabin without any cutaways, camera tricks, or special effects.

Rin-Tin-Tin continued to prove his skill and intelligence over the next eight years as he starred in over thirty films, both silent and sound, saved Warner Brothers from possible bankruptcy, and changed the fate of what became one of the most popular and recognizable breeds of dog in the world.

Rin-Tin-Tin poses with trainer Lee Duncan in 1925. (Author's collection)

His Master's Voice (1925)

GSD: Thunder as himself

Trainer: Frank Foster Davis

Director: Renaud Hoffman

Costars: George Hackathorne, Marjorie Daw

Country: USA

Status: Limited availability

Gotham was one of many Hollywood studios to try its luck with German Shepherd stars in the shadow of Strongheart and Rin-Tin-Tin. One such star was Thunder, billed as "The Marvel Dog," owned and trained by Frank Davis, who also wrote the stories for Thunder's films. A tall, handsome dog, Thunder resembled Strongheart and achieved some success, though not so much as the latter. He starred in five films for Gotham (1924–1927), as well as two for Fox (1926–1927). In reviewing Thunder's first film, *Black Lightning* (1924), costarring Clara Bow, *Variety* praised the dog star by saying, "The picture holds tension through Thunder's splendid work. . . ."

Set during World War I, *His Master's Voice* begins with Thunder and his son, Flash, sitting together on a sunny window seat. A text card appears, reading: "Thunder had seen Life, had faced Death, made sacrifices and won glory, and now, in peaceful retirement, taught his son the qualities essential to a good dog—courage, love, loyalty."

What follows is Thunder's story to Flash of his war dog days. Thunder's master, Bob Barry (George Hackathorne), wishes to study architecture and marry Mary Blake (Marjorie Daw), but finds both plans disrupted by Jack (Brooks Benedict), who taunts Bob for his cowardice. When Bob is drafted, Thunder is also recruited as a Red Cross dog and ultimately saves Bob's life when Bob must reattach a severed explosive's wire in no man's land. While Bob's sole contribution to fixing the wire is crawling toward it, Thunder stops an enemy soldier from sneaking up on him, reconnects the wire himself when Bob is wounded, then drags his master to safety. Why the men didn't send Thunder to do the job in the first place is not explained. Both Bob and Thunder receive medals for bravery and go home to settle the score with Jack.

Wolfheart's Revenge (1925)

GSD: Wolfheart as himself
Trainer: Unknown
Director: Charles R. Seeling
Costars: Guinn "Big Boy" Williams, Kathleen Collins
Country: USA
Status: Rare

Wolfheart's Revenge would be more aptly named *Jack Stanley's Revenge*, as the title character in this case has very little to do with the story. Wolfheart, "The Dog Wonder," plays a passive role in this film, accompanying his master, Jack Stanley ("Big Boy" Williams), on his rounds as a ranch hand at the Star Bar Ranch, owned by Richard Bronson (Captain Bingham).

Richard sends his new foreman, Blackie Blake (Larry Fisher), to offer his neighbors a $5,000 check in return for rights to their water for cattle. When the neighbor refuses, Blackie plants the agreement in his pocket, then shoots him in the back. Blackie frames Jack for cattle rustling and implicates him in the murder before Blackie's men haul Jack off to be hung. Wolfheart brings evidence of Blackie's evil doings to Richard's attention, and Richard stops the hanging in time for Jack to apprehend Blackie, who has kidnapped Richard's niece and Jack's love interest, Betty (Kathleen Collins). Blackie ties Wolfheart to a tree, but the dog frees himself (off screen) in time to knock Blackie into the river.

Wolfheart, a smallish, black sable Shepherd, gives a very forgettable performance here and, after half a dozen films, all in 1925, he vanished into obscurity. Guinn Williams, the leading human in all of Wolfheart's films, continued his acting career, mostly in westerns, until his death in 1962. He had over 200 credits to his name.

The Call of the Wilderness (1926)

GSD: Sandow as him-/herself
Trainer: Earl Johnson
Director: Jack Nelson
Costars: Lewis Sargent, Edna Marion
Country: USA
Status: Rare

Sandow gets top billing here as "Screenland's Greatest Sensation," and in another film, *Avenging Fangs* (1927), was called "America's Greatest Police Dog"—lofty claims for a dog whose career ended after only three films. This is a shame, however, since Sandow really was a good canine actor, interacting very believably with human costars, as well as showing off great physical abilities. Though Sandow plays a male in all three films, he was really a she—and one of the only female GSDs to star in early films.

When Andrew Horton (Lewis Sargent) is told to get out by his wealthy father (Sydney De Gray), Andy heads west with his dog, Sandow. He buys a homestead, drawn not by the land but by the land agent's daughter, Dorothy (Edna Marion). "Red" Morgan (Al Smith), has already found gold on the land and starts trouble with Andy. Andy has no chance when Red takes a swing at him and it's Sandow who drives Red away. When Red plants a log in the road that causes Andy's car to roll into a ravine, Sandow runs to Dorothy for help, assists in digging Andy out, then takes off after Red, forcing him off a cliff to his death—because canine heroes of the 1920s were too refined to ever kill a villain with their teeth.

Earl Johnson, who later became well known for supplying German Shepherds in Hollywood through the 1950s, wrote the story as well in this case. Sandow was a large (for a female), short-coated sable who had many key scenes in this, her second film. Leaping through an open window when the bad guy was waiting at the door, jumping onto countertops and into her master's arms, pulling a baby carriage, carrying a bottle, and attacking the villain to save her master were a few of the feats she had to perform in *The Call of the Wilderness*. In addition, she was smart enough to talk, getting multiple dialogue cards to herself in the film. As she barks to her master, a card shifts from "Woof! Woof!" to "Sure thing— let's go!" Although the film is disturbing to watch due to its pervasive racism, it is worth a look just for Sandow's performance.

The Return of Grey Wolf (1926)

GSD: Leader as *Grey Wolf*
Trainer: Rennie Renfro (unconfirmed)
Director: Jacques Rollens
Costars: James Pierce, Helen Lynch
Country: USA
Status: Rare

Leader's career was even shorter than Sandow's: *The Return of Grey Wolf* was his only film. A far more famous canine appears alongside him here: Buster, a brindle and white mutt who resembled a Basenji and later went on to star in *Anybody's War* (1930), *Lucky Dog* (1933), and the *Dogville Comedies*, a series of 1930s short films made by Metro-Goldwyn-Mayer with all-dog casts that spoofed popular feature films of the time. He was one of the most famous canines of Rennie Renfro's Motion Picture Dogs, a trainer and company known for supplying literally hundreds of dogs for film in the 1920s and 1930s. Although Leader was likely also trained by Rennie Renfro, this is not certain.

The film opens with Grey Wolf (Leader) meeting a gang of dogs, including Buster as Oscar and a German Shepherd puppy, and sitting down with them to tell his story. The dogs speak to each other with dialogue cards, exactly as the human actors did at the time. At the beginning of Leader's story, he runs away from an abusive master and finds the kindly trapper, Louis (James Pierce), and his girlfriend, Jean (Helen Lynch). Jean returns to town, and Grey Wolf (named by Louis) runs off to answer a wolf howl. Then the powder in Louis's rifle explodes in his face, blinding him. Evil Gaston Pacot (Walter Shumway) steals Louis's furs to sell. Louis uses Grey Wolf to guide him to town, looking more like a zombie than a blind man. Grey Wolf gets Louis, who later regains his vision, safely to town, and when Gaston gets the upper hand in the inevitable fight, Grey Wolf attacks Gaston and saves the day.

Though the first real guide dog film, *Wings in the Dark*, was not made until 1936, Leader demonstrated ten years earlier that a good GSD can guide any human hero to victory.

Peter the Great gets the attention of June Marlowe in a publicity shot. (Author's collection)

The Sign of the Claw (1926)

GSD: Peter the Great as himself

Trainer: Edward Faust

Director: B. Reeves Eason

Costars: Edward Hearn, Ethel Shannon

Country: USA

Status: Limited availability

Billed as "The Miracle Dog of the Movies" and "King of the Silver Screen," it seems that Peter the Great had the highest expectations to live up to of all silent GSD stars. Originally a working sheepdog, Peter, like Strongheart and Rin-Tin-Tin, was an immigrant from Europe. He was extremely intelligent and did stunts for other canine stars such as Strongheart and Thunder. Although it was rumored that he performed stunts for Rin-Tin-Tin, this is unlikely since Lee Duncan kept a kennel of German Shepherds who played backup for the Wonder Dog.

The Sign of the Claw has Peter playing a police dog alongside his "pal and master," Bob Conway (Edward Hearn). The two are on the trail of bank robbers: specifically, their ringleader, Al Stokes (Lee Shumway). The relatively complicated plot involves a flashback to Bob's rescue of Peter from the cruel hands of his original master, Al, before the bad guy reclaims Peter during the course of the movie. A good guy, Jimmy (Joe Bennett), is mixed up with the thieves, and a few humans appear almost as smart as the dog, though it's still Peter who saves lives and catches thieves.

Peter the Great was trained by Edward Faust who co-owned him with his brother, Arlis Faust, and Charles B. Dreyer. Peter earned $1,000 a week, plus royalties on his films. He starred in about half a dozen movies, notably *The Silent Accuser* (1924) and *Wild Justice* (1925), not to mention all the films he doubled in, such as Strongheart's *The Love Master* (1924).

In the summer of 1926, when Peter was being called the greatest animal star in the world, he was under contract for six more features—but they were never made. On June 6, 1926, Edward Faust got into an argument with a friend, Fred Cyriacks. The enraged Cyriacks fired his rifle at Faust's car, hitting Peter, who was inside. After three days in the hospital,

Peter died. In late 1927, Faust was awarded $125,000 in court after a lawsuit against Cyriacks. There has been speculation that, had Peter lived longer, he might have achieved as much longstanding fame as Rin-Tin-Tin. Yet although he was an amazing performer, it was his tragic death that set Peter apart in history.

The Return of Boston Blackie (1927)

GSD: Strongheart as himself
Trainer: Laurence Trimble
Director: Harry O. Hoyt
Costars: Bob Custer, Corliss Palmer
Country: USA
Status: Rare

Although still a large and attractive dog, Strongheart was entering his golden years by the time his last movie, *The Return of Boston Blackie*, was made. The noble canine receives top billing above the title, even though his part was relatively small.

At the beginning of the film, Boston Blackie (Bob Custer, credited with his birth name of Raymond Glenn) is being released from prison and reunites with his dog, Strongheart. He tells his old partner (Corliss Palmer) that he has given up his life of crime, but it's not long before he and Strongheart are mixed up in a theft. Blackie and Strongheart take a stolen necklace from a woman on the run from the police in order to protect her. They hide at the Santa Monica Pier, where Strongheart leaps from a towering swing ride into the water below. After both return home, Strongheart is captured by an angry hot-dog vender, whom the dog has been stealing from, and Blackie tries to return the necklace to its owner. Blackie's former partner takes the necklace and gets away right under the noses of the police. Strongheart escapes from a net and a burning building and chases him down.

Besides his films, Strongheart was immortalized through books and publicity including portraits. One appeared on *Classic* magazine and another, by famed wildlife painter Charles Livingston Bull, was on one of the first English language books about German Shepherds, *The Police Dog* by David Brockwell. Brockwell also dedicates this book to Strongheart.

In a 1924 article from *The New York Times*, Strongheart's bark is described as being "like a clap of thunder," yet that bark never made it to his film audience's ears: Strongheart died on June 24, 1929, without ever having appeared in a talkie. The *Times* obituary refers to him as a "Dog Hero of Films." His film legacy lived on for many years in his grandsons, Lightning and Silver King—the former being one of the most successful canine stars of the 1930s and the latter motivating children to stay safe with the Silver King Safety Club. Strongheart is still remembered today by fans who know him as the first German Shepherd superstar: the one who started it all.

Tracked by the Police (1927)

GSD: Rin-Tin-Tin as *Satan*
Trainer: Lee Duncan
Director: Ray Enright
Costars: Jason Robards Sr., Virginia Brown Faire
Country: USA
Status: Limited availability

Although all of Rin-Tin-Tin's films were both physically and mentally demanding, *Tracked by the Police* seemed to go above and beyond what any reasonable writer or director could expect a dog to do: leaping both into and out of a 10-foot-deep pit, climbing a two-story ladder onto a rooftop, hiding inside a grandfather clock, sneaking through rafters, racing across a narrow platform over a rushing river, and turning, pulling, and pushing knobs and levers made of wood and metal. But Rin-Tin-Tin did it all—without special effects or cutaways.

The plot involves Rin-Tin-Tin and his master, Dan Owen (Jason Robards), trying to protect a dam from sabotage. Marcella Bradley (Virginia Brown Faire) arrives with her dog, Princess Beth (Nanette, who was Rin-Tin-Tin's

"TRACKED BY THE POLICE" *starring* RIN-TIN-TIN – A Warner Bros Production

Rin-Tin-Tin (left) with Nanette on the set of *Tracked by the Police.*
(Author's collection)

mate in real life—not to be confused with his deceased sister—and appeared in several films with him). When Dan is shot by Michael Sturgeon (Tom Santschi) and falls through floorboards into a pit, Rin-Tin-Tin rushes a message to Marcella, though he himself is shot on the way. She hides him in a grandfather clock when the villains come for him, and he escapes. Soon, he must choose between saving Marcella or Princess Beth from the rapids Michael and his men have unleashed. He chooses "duty over love" and rescues Marcella, then finds Princess Beth alive once he has stopped the rapids.

Over and over in his dozens of films, Rin-Tin-Tin registered a range of emotion beyond his human costars. The intensity of his performance in films like *Lighthouse by the Sea* (1924) and *The Night Cry* (1926) is astounding. Receiving 12,000 fan letters each week, earning $6,000 a month, and insured for $100,000, Rin-Tin-Tin made an estimated $5 million for Duncan in his career and was voted the most popular Hollywood star two years running in one poll. He was also the reason cited by Duncan's wife when she divorced him.

Rin-Tin-Tin's acting ability was, and still is, unmatched by any other canine performer, and his death on August 10, 1932, was national news. After his death, he was returned to his birthplace of France and buried at Cimetière des Chiens, near Paris.

The Law's Lash (1928)

GSD: Klondike as *Scout*
Trainer: Earl Johnson
Director: Noel M. Smith
Costars: Robert Ellis, Mary Mayberry
Country: USA
Status: Rare

Klondike, a black sable who resembled Sandow, shared a trainer with the latter as well. It is likely, though not certain, that these two were related. Klondike appears to be more of a "trick" dog than Sandow. Without the skills of Rin-Tin-Tin, Peter the Great, or even Thunder, Klondike does at least outstrip Wolfheart with his acting ability. Throughout *The Law's Lash*, he wears a handsome, studded, leather harness which differentiates him from his competitors.

Scout (Klondike) is investigating fur thieves with his Northwest Mounted Police owner, Constable Maloney (Jack Marsh), when Maloney is shot and killed, leaving only a scrap of wood with a final message that reveals his murderer and Scout as a witness. Scout helps Ted (Robert Ellis) and the other Mounties bring the villains to justice. Scout has his work cut out for him, as Ted's friends are a slow lot, but in the end, Scout prevails.

One of the most entertaining scenes in *The Law's Lash* is Klondike's rescue of Margery (Mary Mayberry) from the villains, when she has been locked in a closet. The man on guard hears Scout at the door to the cabin and opens it to get rid of the dog. Instead, Scout drives him back into the cabin. To defend himself, the man grabs the chair that was keeping the door closed on Margery. As soon as the chair is gone, Margery throws open the door, Scout forces the man back into the closet, and Margery locks him in. This is all shot as a single, wide-angle sequence without cuts—something that would be a great rarity in a dog film today.

One-sheet movie poster from *Tracked*. Note that Ranger is the only credited member of the cast. (Author's collection)

Tracked (1928)

GSD: Ranger as himself

Trainer: Unknown

Director: Jerome Storm

Costars: Sam Nelson, Caryl Lincoln

Country: USA

Status: Limited availability

Ranger was a lean, short-coated dog who closely resembled a modern day Belgian Malinois. Although critics did not care for him (saying he could not act, could not fight, and had a substandard supporting cast), he made up for quality with quantity, starring in at least sixteen films from 1926 to

1929, which made him one of the top-producing GSD stars of silent films. Note that critics' reference to the supporting cast for a dog indicates how seriously the canine stars of the time were thought of.

In *Tracked*, one of Ranger's later films, the overused story line finds the star being falsely accused of sheep killing. When he is sentenced to death, his master, Jed Springer (Sam Nelson), hides him from the other ranchers, hoping to find the real killer. Ranger repays him by saving Molly (Caryl Lincoln)—who is coming home from boarding school to visit her father (Clark Comstock)—from a runaway carriage. Ranger races after the horses, catches the reins, brings them to a stop, then fetches Jed to help the fainted Molly. When Jed finds Ranger over the body of a sheep, he thinks the worst and resigns himself to shooting the dog, as per the ranchers' law. At the last minute, Molly spots the real killer and rushes to stop Jed.

The harsh reviews of Ranger seem unwarranted when watching his performance in *Tracked*. He displays a gamut of emotions when his master becomes the firing squad: first, excitement at seeing him, then slowly turning his head away as he realizes something is wrong, lying down, holding up a paw, and finally crawling to Jed's feet, where he gazes upward with apparently grief-stricken eyes.

Under the Black Eagle (1928)

GSD: Flash as *Prinz*

Trainer: William Frederick Steuer

Director: W.S. Van Dyke

Costars: Ralph Forbes, Marceline Day

Country: USA

Status: Unknown

MGM tried three different German Shepherd stars in an effort to compete with Warner Brothers' Rin-Tin-Tin. First, Peter the Great in *The Silent Accuser* (1924), then Napoleon in *The Thirteenth Hour* (1927), and a year later, Flash, a light-colored, short-coated, tall dog with a striking face. Flash proved to be a hit in *Under the Black Eagle* and was cast shortly thereafter in *Shadows of the Night* and *Honeymoon*, both also made in 1928.

Similar to *His Master's Voice* (see page 9), *Under the Black Eagle* is the story of a young man, Karl (Ralph Forbes), who is drafted during World War I but has no wish to fight. He leaves behind his loyal dog, Prinz (Flash), and his girlfriend, Margarta (Marceline Day). Like Thunder, Prinz arrives on the battlefield in time to save the day: carrying a message through no man's land, saving Karl's life, and being wounded himself before both Prinz and Karl can return to Margarta.

MGM's promotional herald for *Under the Black Eagle* claimed that it was "The greatest dog film ever made!" Dozens of different publicity stills were issued of Flash, including poses with the cubs of MGM's iconic lion, Leo, and he was billed as "MGM's Famous Police Dog." But Flash's fame was not to last. He only made three films with MGM, and it wasn't until 1933 that he came back to the screen for another feature, made by Imperial Productions, called *The Flaming Signal* (see page 31).

Flash poses on a tennis court with actress Lucille Williams in 1928. (Author's collection)

Wilderness Tails: The 1930s

By the 1930s, the German Shepherd Dog had become one of the most popular and widely recognized breeds in the United States, due largely to their silver screen presence. As the Great Depression swept the country, people who had nothing still went to the cinema: a child could get into a movie for 10 cents and an adult for 25 cents or less. While the country was hurting, Hollywood was racing to keep up with the demand for more films.

Even Rin-Tin-Tin continued performing until 1931, his last film, *The Lightning Warrior*, being a twelve-chapter serial. His sons and grandsons took over in 1932 and went on outsmarting everyone else in their movies for years to come. Now, however, the dogs were at a disadvantage: human actors could speak. Also, trainers who had once been able to talk to their dogs while cameras rolled now often had to remain silent. Despite interest in canine performers beginning to dwindle with the addition of sound to all theatrical films, dozens of studios still produced hundreds of dog movies during the 1930s. Many of them followed a variety of wilderness themes and were often less sophisticated and not as well made as the silent films had been.

Trailing the Killer (1932)

Also known as *Call of the Wilderness*
GSD: Caesar as *Lobo*
Trainer: Unknown
Director: Herman C. Raymaker
Costars: Francis McDonald, Heinie Conklin
Country: USA
Status: Available on DVD

Trailing the Killer is one of many obvious examples demonstrating why the American Humane Association—not to be confused with the American Humane Society—began monitoring animal action on movie sets beginning in 1940, though it was too late to help Caesar and his canine and feline costars. Even at the time, audiences were sympathetic to Caesar's plight; a *New York Times* review said, "He unfortunately has to submit to some unpleasant experiences. . . ." though the reviewer liked the film overall and went on to say that Caesar was "one of the handsomest dogs that have taken up motion picture work."

Caesar plays a wolf-dog named Lobo who divides his time between his trapper master, Pierre LaPlant (Francis MacDonald), and his wolf mate (a Siberian Husky). Accused of sheep killing by farmers, Lobo finds the real killer, a cougar. LaPlant discovers the body of a sheep and also believes Lobo to be the guilty one. He is about to shoot Lobo when the cat springs on him and kills him. Finding Lobo with the body later, the farmers think he killed his master. Lobo escapes with a $100 bounty on his head. He eventually tracks the cougar down and clears his own name, freeing his mate from a trap and rescuing his puppies from the cat along the way. The entire family is adopted by one of the farmers after Lobo saves his life from the killer cat.

The methods used to obtain most of the animal footage here were stressful and often painful or dangerous to the performers. When Caesar kills a rattlesnake to protect his puppies, a stunt double for the dog and a real snake were used. To create the look of howling, both Caesar and the husky playing his mate had wires fastened around their lower jaws that were pulled sharply upward. The struggle of his mate in a leg-hold trap, and Caesar being caught in a hanging trap, are painful to watch. The cougar fares no better than the dogs, appearing underfed, stressed, and frightened in every shot.

The Flaming Signal (1933)

GSD: Flash as himself
Trainer: William Frederick Steuer
Directors: George Jeske, Charles Edward Roberts
Costars: John David Horsley, Marceline Day
Country: USA
Status: Available on DVD

After his stint as a silent film star with Metro-Goldwyn-Mayer, Flash returned in one feature film, *The Flaming Signal*, for Imperial Productions, as well as a series of shorts, until 1935. Flash went on for a final big-screen performance in Republic Pictures' 1938 *Call the Mesquiteers*. In his last film, he is only seen at the end, helping his humans out of a jam, and you can tell he is getting older.

When Lieutenant Robbins (John David Horsley) attempts a historic solo flight to the Hawaiian Islands, his plane is thrown off course in a storm and catches on fire. Robbins's dog, Flash, who had the forethought to bring his own parachute, jumps to safety. He plunges into the ocean to save Robbins from the crashed plane. They find themselves on Tabu Island, where they meet Sally James (Marceline Day). She takes them to her home and father, Reverend James (Henry B. Walthall). The native islanders are being oppressed by evil trading post owner Otto Von Krantz (Noah Beery). After Von Krantz shoots the native chief, the remaining villagers turn against Robbins, Reverend James, and his daughter. Robbins spends much of the film with the same expression on his face—mixed amusement and surprise—regardless of what is going on. Flash does the heavy lifting; running a burning torch to the top of a hill to set off a signal fire, taking down Von Krantz, and saving Robbins and Sally James from a spear-carrying villager.

It seems surprising that Flash did not star in more films, especially early in his career. If he could not get any better deals than *The Flaming Signal*, however, it is probably best that he did not. He is given top billing in this film both at the opening and end credits. Since the story itself does not center around him, one can only assume this was because the producers realized he was their best actor.

Jaws of Justice (1933)

GSD: Kazan as himself
Trainer: Unknown
Director: Spencer Gordon Bennet
Costars: Richard Terry, Ruth Sullivan
Country: USA
Status: Available on DVD

The long-disappeared production company behind *Jaws of Justice*, Sol Lesser Productions, was responsible for many other animal-related movies, including *Fighting to Live* (1934, with GSDs Captain and Lady), *Ferocious Pal* (1934, also starring Kazan), *Peck's Bad Boy with the Circus* (1938), and more than fifteen different *Tarzan* films. Kazan was one of a few German Shepherd stars to be involved with the company at some point and was probably their best known canine star. He was not as skilled as Flash, nor as attractive, with a very long, sharp face and a docked tail. His attack scenes consist mostly of being pulled around by an actor in an effort to make it look as though the dog is savaging him, yet the film tagline stated he was a "dog that outacts a man!"

It is likely, though unconfirmed, that Kazan was bred and raised for police work. It was not uncommon at the time for such working German Shepherds to have their tails docked, and the practice continues today for some working police K-9s. As far back as the GSD's original German standard, docked tails were highly faulted, and the dog with a docked tail was considered unacceptable for breeding. The earliest German Shepherd Dog Club of America and American Kennel Club standards list a docked tail as a disqualification.

Jaws of Justice centers largely around a sergeant in the Royal Canadian Mounted Police. Surprisingly, he is not Kazan's master in the film. That role goes to a young, mute man (Gene Toler, credited as Jean Toller) who is a friend of Sergeant Kinkaid (Richard Terry) and has another dog named Lightnin' Teddy (a mixed breed). Kinkaid falls for Judy Dean (Ruth Sullivan) before her father heads off to register a gold claim with the Canadian government. He never makes the claim but is murdered en route. Kazan is the only witness but fails to communicate what he has seen to the good guy humans. Once Kinkaid does uncover the murder and the culprit, Kazan has a shining moment as he chews through a rope that the bad guy is trying to climb and puts out a burning fuse.

Inside Information (1934)

GSD: Tarzan (see description)
Trainer: Earl Johnson (unconfirmed)
Director: Robert F. Hill
Costars: Rex Lease, Marion Shilling
Country: USA
Status: Limited availability

Tarzan "The Police Dog" appeared in a few films during 1934 and 1935, the same time Lightning began his career. Tarzan and Lightning were the same size and color, had the same markings, did the same kinds of stunts, and appear to have had the same temperament and level of drive. While it is easy to trace Lightning, Strongheart's grandson, back to trainer Earl Johnson and find numerous articles on him, Tarzan is more of a mystery. Without positive proof either way, it is impossible to say whether Lightning and Tarzan were actually the same dog. If the two were not the same dog, it seems fairly certain at least that both worked under the same trainer and were probably close relatives (such as brothers).

Inside Information opens with Lloyd Wilson (Rex Lease) arguing for his dog, Tarzan, to be given a badge of honor. The police commissioner (Henry Roquemore) tells him bestowing such a thing on a dog is out of the question. Wilson asks that he at least be allowed to tell the dog's story. What follows is a tale of Tarzan's heroic retrieval of stolen bank bonds, the loss of which had been blamed on his owner. Among the film's many flaws are the frequent asides into other people's perspectives, including the thieves' and Tarzan's, although the story is supposedly being told by Wilson. *Inside Information* concludes very abruptly with the return to the police station, where Tarzan is awaiting the commissioner's decision. Wilson's story has wrapped up with the dog being shot through the paw, though not a drop of blood is seen.

If any reader has evidence to settle the question of the Lightning/Tarzan connection, the author would be grateful to hear from you through the website found on the back of this book.

Lightning poses for a publicity shot. (Author's collection)

When Lightning Strikes (1934)

GSD: Lightning as himself

Trainer: Earl Johnson

Directors: Burton King, Harry Revier

Costars: Ralph Bushman, Alice Dahl

Country: USA

Status: Rare

Six years after Strongheart's death, his grandson appeared as the title character in *The Case of the Howling Dog* (1934). A few months later, Lightning starred in *When Lightning Strikes*. In this, he receives top billing and became established as "The Wonder Dog." Sherman S. Krellberg formed Regal Distributing Corporation specifically to make films starring the talented dog. He planned on three other Lightning films produced from 1934 to 1935. What really happened: the company made one more GSD film, *Thunderbolt* (1935, starring Lobo, not Lightning), then went bankrupt.

There is not much plot to speak of in this film—it is more of a series of chases and rescues involving Lightning on both the giving and receiving end. The predictable handsome, wilderness-savvy dog owner, some ruffian villains, and a beautiful young woman are all caught in a land dispute involving lumber rights. Lightning is in the thick of it, delivering paperwork, saving his master from a burning building, and rooting out bad guys.

According to a press release, Lightning was six months old when he began work on *When Lightning Strikes*. This is not true, although he certainly was young. Trainer Earl Johnson had been prepping the puppy for film work since his first weeks of life. Lightning earned a reputation for performing complex scenes after one or two rehearsals and with minimal direction from his trainer. Like Rin-Tin-Tin, Lightning had a family that was the subject of press interest, including his mate, Silver Queen, and son, Lightning Jr. He also had his own stand-in, a dog named Gary. Promotions for *When Lightning Strikes* claimed, "Lightning . . . surpasses in intelligence all the dog stars previously seen on the talking screen." And, "Lightning's part in the story could well have been played by a human being, so quickly does the dog's mind seem to work."

Courage of the North (1935)

GSD: Captain as himself

Trainer: Unknown

Director: Robert Emmett Tansey

Costars: John Preston, June Love

Country: USA

Status: Limited availability

Captain, along with the starring horse of the film, Dynamite (also the name of a GSD star), received this immortal advertising in press materials from Stage and Screen:

"Both 'Dynamite' and 'Captain,' are without a shadow of a doubt the most intelligent and praiseworthy animals who have yet made appearances on the silver screen."

His publicist went on to say that Captain was destined to "displace Strongheart and Rin-Tin-Tin as the most popular canine actor of all time." Notice that Strongheart was still well known in 1935, eight years after his last film. Though he starred in many adventure films, Captain was not so well remembered.

In *Courage of the North*, Sergeant Bruce Morton (John Preston) of the Northwest Mounted Police sets off in search of fur thieves with his Wonder Horse, Dynamite; Captain, "King of Dogs"; and Corporal Jimmy Downs (Jimmy Aubrey). On their way, Bruce rescues Yvonne Travis (June Love) from rapids after her canoe turns over. Back in her own town, Yvonne and her father are being bullied by Mordant (William Desmond), who wants to marry her, but he withdraws at sight of Bruce's uniform. Mordant and his men capture Bruce and Jimmy, leaving them tied in an old trapper shack set with explosives. Captain and Dynamite come to the rescue, breaking in and setting the men free in time to escape. Mordant kidnaps Yvonne after killing her father and makes an unsuccessful getaway as Bruce and his four-footed companions save the day.

The Test (1935)

GSD: Rin Tin Tin Jr. as *Rinnie*
Trainer: Lee Duncan
Director: Bernard B. Ray
Costars: Grant Withers, Grace Ford
Country: USA
Status: Available on DVD

Based on a James Oliver Curwood story, as many of Rin Tin Tin Jr.'s films were, *The Test* stars one of several dogs who played Rin Tin Tin Jr. in over a dozen feature films and three twelve-chapter serials. Note that while the original Rin-Tin-Tin's name was usually spelled with hyphens, these were almost always dropped for Rin Tin Tin Jr.

When evil Pepite La Joie (Monte Blue) steals furs trapped by Brule Conway (Grant Withers), Rinnie (Rin Tin Tin Jr.) finds the furs and gets them back for his master. Conway leaves Rinnie to guard the furs while he goes to sort things out with La Joie. Why he does this is unclear since he could easily take the furs with him. After Conway has driven them out of town, the bad guys lure Rinnie away from guard duty to steal the furs by using Nanette, a cream-colored GSD puppy. When Conway finds the furs gone, Beth McVey (Grace Ford) convinces him to give the dog another chance and tells Rinnie to bring them back. Much of the rest of the film is Rinnie's tracking, stalking, tricking, and attacking the bad guys himself until his master at last catches up to him and all four are together: Rinnie, Nanette, Conway, and McVey.

Canine actors are not necessarily the bold and determined protectors in real life that we are shown on screen. A *New York Times* news article from one year after *The Test* was released states that Rin Tin Tin Jr. was at home during a break-in and robbery at Lee Duncan's house: the thieves reportedly stole over $500 in jewelry and clothing while the German Shepherd celebrity slept.

Several different dogs played not only stunt doubles for Rin Tin Tin Jr., but the main dog's part in different films. However, every dog playing him was a son or grandson of the original Rin-Tin-Tin. Lee Duncan continued to breed from the line until his death in 1960. The Rin-Tin-Tin line survives today.

White Fang (1936)

GSD: Lightning as *White Fang*
Trainer: Earl Johnson
Director: David Butler
Costars: Michael Whalen, Jean Muir
Country: USA
Status: Rare

Lightning had made a name for himself by the time *White Fang* was released in 1936. In 1935, he starred in *A Dog of Flanders* and acted alongside Cary Grant in *Wings in the Dark*. *Wings in the Dark* was the first ever guide dog film. Lightning received a private coach from The Seeing Eye school to help prep him for the role. Though *White Fang* was disappointing, bearing no resemblance to Jack London's novel other than the dog's name, it is fitting that Lightning appeared in it since his grandfather, Strongheart, starred in the original *White Fang* film of 1925. Lightning puts in a great performance, which was praised in both *The New York Times* and *The Los Angeles Times*—the latter even said he would give Buck a run for his money.

When Gordon Scott (Michael Whalen) guides Hal Burgess (Thomas Beck) through the frozen north, he tells him the legend of a super dog who returned to the wild—Buck from *The Call of the Wild* (1935)—and of the super dog's son, White Fang. Wolves eat the men's sled team. The two have almost succumbed to hunger when Burgess kills himself. Scott collapses in the snow and is watched over by White Fang (Lightning). Natives find Scott and take him to Caribou Creek, where Burgess had a gold claim he inherited from his uncle. Scott convinces the authorities that he is Burgess and the mine is his. The scam goes well until Scott gets on the wrong side of the local bad guy by rescuing White Fang from a dogfight. Then Burgess's sister arrives in town and Scott is accused of murdering the man he has been impersonating.

A double was used for Lightning in the fight scene, along with an American Pit Bull Terrier. Both wore tight muzzles made from a single strand of wire that looped their jaws and ran around behind their ears. The scene is quite disturbing as the fighting was not faked. In one moment, the GSD is thrown on his back into the center of the ring from off camera, and the APBT drives into his stomach while he's still down, using the weight of his body to pin the other dog and trying to bite through his muzzle.

Topa Topa (1937)

Also known as *Children of the Wild*
GSD: Silver Wolf as *Fang* (*Fangs* in credits, but called *Fang*)
Trainer: Louis Vokali
Directors: Charles Hutchison, Vin Moore
Costars: Joan Valerie, James Bush
Country: USA
Status: Available on DVD

Silver Wolf has a fitting screen name in *Topa Topa*, which is more widely known as *Children of the Wild*. Showing his teeth in alarming snarls was a specialty for him. Though he appeared in other films, including the 1937 serial *Radio Patrol*, *Topa Topa* was Silver Wolf's most demanding film, with *Call of the Yukon* (see next entry) a close second.

Silver Wolf shows his gentle side. The identity of his child friend is unknown. (Author's collection)

The story is something of a mix between *Trailing the Killer* (see page 29) and Rin-Tin-Tin's *The Night Cry* (1926). Jim Turner (James Bush) and Margaret Weston (Joan Valerie) are planning their future together after he saves her from drowning. Then a man is murdered and a dog is blamed, of course. Revisiting a plot line from Silver Wolf's first film, *The Rogues' Tavern* (1936), the killer, Pete (LeRoy Mason), uses a taxidermic canine head to plant bite marks on the victim, and Fang (Silver Wolf) ends up with a price on his head. The moment to redeem himself comes when a golden eagle (Goldie) swoops down and carries away a toddler to her cliff-front nest. (No comment.) Fang has a showdown with the bird and watches over the little girl along with his own puppies, who lost their mother in a forest fire. He even steals a can of milk from a nearby cabin and opens it for her before they are found by Jim.

Though the story is a rather tired one, Silver Wolf, a medium-sized, black sable dog, makes the film worth seeing. Silver Wolf's trainer, Louis Vokali, made a brief appearance as an evil henchman in *Radio Patrol*. Vokali was also responsible for a GSD star of the silent screen, Fearless. Fearless performed in a series of twelve short films about "Fearless, the Dog Detective" in 1926 and one in 1927, all produced by Van Pelt Productions and with titles like *Detective K-9*, *Dog of Dogs*, and *Almost Human*.

Call of the Yukon (1938)

GSD: Silver Wolf as *Swift Lightning*
Trainer: Louis Vokali
Directors: B. Reeves Eason, John T. Coyle
Costars: Beverly Roberts, Richard Arlen
Country: USA
Status: Available on DVD

Directed by B. Reeves Eason, who also worked with Peter the Great, and based on the novel *Swift Lightning*, by James Oliver Curwood, *Call of the Yukon* is a disturbing film on many levels, from its male chauvinist leading man to the pervading depictions of cruelly treated animals. Then there are the memorable lines like this one: "He's just a half-breed wolf-dog. Cross a dog with a wolf and you get a super dog or a super wolf, but always a killer."

Jean Williams (Beverly Roberts), a writer, refuses to leave the small native village where she's been living in Alaska, even when famine drives out everyone else. At last the only ones left are her, a trapper named Gaston (Richard Arlen), and Jean's animal companions—bears, a raven, and a Collie named Firefly. Jean and Gaston leave the village for Nenana, followed by a pack of starving wild dogs who are headed by Swift Lightning (Silver Wolf). Jean has a soft spot for the "wolf-dog" even before he befriends Firefly and digs Jean out after an avalanche, but Gaston wants to shoot him. When they lose their sled team and food in breaking river ice, Gaston tries to kill and eat Firefly but Swift Lightning rushes to her aid. Paralleling stories are drawn between the relationship of Swift Lightning and Firefly, and that of Gaston and Jean. The refined Hugo (Lyle Talbot) and his "gentleman" dog, Buck, are juxtaposed next to the uncivilized males.

The whole second half of the opening cast credits for *Call of the Yukon* is animals. They are listed as follows: "Swift Lightning, Firefly, Buck, Toughie and Roughie, Winkey." The last three are bears and a raven, and the most famous is Buck, the Saint Bernard star of *The Call of the Wild* with Clark Gable. Trainer Carl Spitz, best known for training Terry, the dog who played Toto in *The Wizard of Oz* (1939), was one of the most prolific and well-respected Hollywood trainers of the 1930s. He presumably trained Firefly as well.

Orphans of the Street (1938)

GSD: Ace as *Skippy*
Trainer: Earl Johnson
Director: John H. Auer
Costars: Tommy Ryan, Robert Livingston
Country: USA
Status: Rare

Ace was literally born to be a star. The son of Lightning and great-grandson of Strongheart, Ace, registered as Silver Tips, originally went by the call name Lightning Jr. until his first film, *Blind Alibi* (1938), which was released seven months before *Orphans of the Street*. The script called for a German Shepherd named Ace playing opposite Richard Dix. Junior got the part and his trainer, Earl Johnson, was so fond of "Ace" that Junior got a new name.

Ace was one of the most prominent German Shepherd actors of his time, starring in well over a dozen films, including the first of the *Rusty* series and multiple James Oliver Curwood adaptations such as *God's Country* (1946). He was featured in *Jack London* (1943), where he played Jack London's dog, and his roles were some of the most diverse of any GSD star: he was a war hero, a police dog, a child's companion, a sled dog, a sci-fi sidekick in a serial; *The Phantom* (1943), and more.

In *Orphans of the Street*, Ace plays Skippy, the companion of an orphaned boy attending military school. When his funding runs out, Tommy (Tommy Ryan) is sent to an orphanage and Skippy is taken from him. Tommy never makes it to the orphanage, however; he runs away to rescue Skippy, then devises a plan to enter Skippy in a dog show with a top prize of $15,000. A reporter gives them a lift to the show, where Tommy finds out Skippy cannot compete without American Kennel Club papers. When show dogs are stolen, Skippy tracks down the bad guy in a graveyard—then the man is found dead and Skippy is accused of the killing. It's up to Tommy and the reporter, Bob Clayton (Robert Livingston), to clear Skippy's name and save his life before it's too late.

Torchy Gets Her Man (1938)

GSD: Cyclone as *Blitzen*
Trainer: Frank Weatherwax
Director: William Beaudine
Costars: Glenda Farrell, Barton MacLane
Country: USA
Status: Rare

Torchy Blane was a female reporter who appeared in a series of nine Warner Brothers films made from 1937 to 1939. The films' characters were based on ones created by Louis Frederick Nebel. Glenda Farrell plays Torchy Blane, the bright and motivated newspaperwoman, determined in all the films to get to the bottom of the story and get it in print. She is aided, though more often hindered, by her detective boyfriend, Steve McBride (Barton MacLane).

In this, the sixth Torchy Blane installment, Torchy teams up with a German Shepherd to track down the bad guys—but only after she had asked for a Bloodhound. Her friend who provides the dog, Gahagan (Tom Kennedy), explains that Blitzen (Cyclone) is a top-of-the-line police dog from Germany: "The way Blitzen can sniff a trail, it'd make a Bloodhound look like he had a cold." Unfortunately, the dog does not know English, so Torchy uses an English-to-German dictionary to communicate. She shows him creosote that she has put on a car tire so he can track it, which he does, leading them to the right house and into a trap. Torchy, Gahagan, and Blitzen are captured. With Torchy's help, Blitzen escapes to fetch backup, bringing a squad of police officers, including Steve, to rescue Torchy and Gahagan before a bomb goes off.

The same dog played Blitzen as starred in the 1928 silent, ten-chapter serial, *The Yellow Cameo*, although the dog in *Torchy Gets Her Man* does not appear to be a senior citizen. Cyclone was trained by Frank and Rudd Weatherwax long before Lassie first came to the screen. The Weatherwax brothers also trained such famous canines as Asta (Skippy) from the *Thin Man* series and Daisy (Spooks) from the *Blondie* series, as well as working with some of Hollywood's best known dog trainers from the 1920s and 1930s; Henry East, Rennie Renfro, and Carl Spitz.

Will the real Rin Tin Tin Jr. please stand up? Here, the registered Junior is seen with Lee Duncan in 1932 (Rin-Tin-Tin in the background), though the many dogs to play him often looked very different. (Courtesy Miss Daphne Hereford)

Law of the Wolf (1939)

GSD: Rin Tin Tin Jr. as *Rinty*

Trainer: Lee Duncan

Director: Bernard B. Ray

Costars: Dennis Moore, Luana Walters

Country: USA

Status: Rare

Rin Tin Tin Jr., this time appearing as a black and cream, stars in this, one of his later films. The difference between the appearance of the various dogs playing Rin Tin Tin Jr. in separate films is startling. While the stunt doubles of some dogs, such as Caesar, are easy to distinguish from the original because of different markings, the dogs still played themselves in all their credited roles. It is unclear why Rin Tin Tin Jr. was the exception to this rule, appearing in films as everything from a tan sable to a black and tan with predominate facial markings to the light-colored and sparingly marked black and cream seen here. The lighter dogs are the ones most often seen in his publicity photos and their is look most often associated with Junior.

In *Law of the Wolf*, which features no wolf, no dog playing a wolf, and no mention of any wolf, Rinty (Rin Tin Tin Jr.) must track down his own master, Carl Pearson (Dennis Moore), for the police after Pearson has escaped from prison. Of course, Pearson—convicted of killing his own brother—is innocent, but his breakout has him in the debt of a murderer who made it possible. After narrow escapes from the law by

Pearson and feats of brilliance by his dog, Pearson makes it to a cabin where valuable plans to an airplane were left by his brother. He at last manages to prove his innocence when the plans are stolen and Rinty must save the day.

One of the Juniors went on to appear as the original Rin-Tin-Tin in *Hollywood Cavalcade* (1939). He plays his father while Lee Duncan plays himself as he tries to get his dog a job in movies. The producer who turns them away (Don Ameche) never hears the end of it after Rin-Tin-Tin comes out on top in popularity polls. In all, Rin Tin Tin Jr. starred in about fifteen features and serials, playing opposite such names as Jackie Cooper in *Tough Guy* (1936) and one of the most famous horses of the silver screen, Rex, in *The Adventures of Rex and Rinty* (1935). Rin Tin Tin Jr. died in 1943 at age twelve. His mate, Treulene, the mother of Rin Tin Tin III, predeceased him: she was a K-9 Corps dog in World War II who was killed in the South Pacific.

Child's Play: The 1940s

The United States emerged from the Great Depression with better budgets and longer shooting schedules. The quality of films improved from the 1930s, but then, like much of the rest of the world, America was once again at war. Movies became flooded with government propaganda about the war. Hollywood German Shepherds did their part by encouraging the public to support such programs as Dogs for Defense.

While there were still plenty of wilderness wolf-dog stories and crime fighting canines in German Shepherd Dog movies, something new was taking over: by the 1940s, movies starring dogs had become primarily thought of as children's films. One of the best known child/dog films ever made was produced in 1943: *Lassie Come Home*. Never again were adults to flock to movie theaters because of a dog's name at the top of a poster (a poster on which no human actor was even credited). There were two recurring themes that dominated GSD films of 1940s America: war hero and boy-and-his-dog. If at all possible, both themes would be squeezed into one film.

Sign of the Wolf (1941)

GSD: Grey Shadow as himself
Trainer: Frank V. Barnes
Director: Howard Bretherton
Costars: Grace Bradley, Michael Whalen
Country: USA
Status: Limited availability

Monogram, the production company, claimed Grey Shadow's first film, *Wolf Call* (1939), was based on Jack London's novel by the same title. However, London wrote no such book. With *Sign of the Wolf*, also by Monogram, the company states that the film is based on London's short story, *That Spot*, about a dog named Spot and two men whom he nearly drives mad while traveling with them in the Yukon. *Sign of the Wolf* not only bares no resemblance to *That Spot*, it does not feature any dog named Spot. In addition, the film follows exactly the same basic premise as Rin Tin Tin Jr.'s 1939 film, *Fangs of the Wild*. Monogram's producers seem to have had a fondness for promoting themselves using the famous author's name, but never took time to read his books.

Grey Shadow, an unusual-looking, black sable shepherd with pale eyes, stars opposite another GSD, Smokey. At the beginning of the film, the two dogs, owned by Judy Weston (Grace Bradley), get into a fight in an obedience ring. Judy sells Shadow and heads for her northern home in a bush plane, but Ben (Mantan Moreland), her assistant, has smuggled Shadow on board. The plane crashes in the wilderness and Shadow races to a fox farm to get help in the form of Rod Freeman (Michael Whalen). Smokey wanders away and is found by fur thieves, who teach him to steal foxes. Shadow takes the blame for the missing foxes and must track down his old kennel-mate to clear his own name.

Frank Barnes owned multiple well known film Shepherds, including Zandra and Flame. Grey Shadow, who appeared in several other films, such as *Wild Geese Calling* (1941), kept his own bank account. A Pathé newsreel from the time showed Grey Shadow purchasing a war bond, taking it home, digging up his safe in the yard, opening it and putting the bond inside, then covering it again. For more on Grey Shadow's involvement with World War II propaganda see *My Pal, Wolf* on page 59.

Eyes in the Night (1942)

GSD: Friday as himself
Trainer: William Frederick Steuer
Director: Fred Zinnemann
Costars: Edward Arnold, Ann Harding
Country: USA
Status: Available on DVD

Based on the novel *The Odor of Violets*, by Baynard Kendrick, *Eyes in the Night* was the first of two films featuring blind detective Duncan Maclain and his German Shepherd guide dog, Friday. The second film, *The Hidden Eye*, was released three years later, and in 2005, a short-lived TV show, *Blind Justice*, touched on the idea again before being canceled after thirteen episodes. *Blind Justice* also costarred a GSD guide dog, Hank, leading the human hero, played by Ron Eldard. Today, few GSDs are being trained as guides, having been replaced by Labrador and Golden Retrievers.

Detective Maclain (Edward Arnold) is demonstrating his fight moves to friends, with Friday's help, when an old acquaintance comes calling: Norma Lawry (Ann Harding). Lawry wants Maclain's aid in getting rid of an unwanted suitor who is after her stepdaughter. Before he does anything, Lawry finds the man dead. Barbara (Donna Reed), the daughter, accuses her stepmother of killing him, and Lawry returns to Maclain with a new request—finding out who did it. What follows is Maclain and Friday's investigation of the case, tracking down clues and playing the blind old uncle to escape detection by the killers. Toward the end, Maclain slips a message into a tube on the dog's collar, which looks like an old military message dog collar, and sends him out a second-story window for help. Friday leaps through high windows, climbs walls, and avoids the temptation of a Standard Poodle on his way.

Friday acts as guide and police dog, though in Baynard Kendrick's books, the blind detective had two German Shepherds: Schnucke, a guide dog, and Dreist, a protection dog. Friday was the son of Flash and had a similar build and short coat. His sable coloring is much darker than his sire's light gold, with only a little black on his muzzle and back. Friday outperforms Flash here, with the fate of the story resting on his shoulders.

War Dogs (1942)

Also known as *Unsung Heroes*
GSD: Ace as *Pal*
Trainer: Earl Johnson
Director: S. Roy Luby
Costars: Billy Lee, Addison Richards
Country: USA
Status: Limited availability

The Dogs for Defense kennel shown in *War Dogs* was filmed at the training kennel of Carl Spitz, whose Hollywood Dog Training School is still running today in North Hollywood. A message precedes the film: *This picture is dedicated to you loyal citizens who unselfishly are enlisting your "Dogs for Defense." For the cooperation in making of WAR DOGS we thank the "Dogs for Defense" organization, and in particular, Consultant to the War Dept., Mr. Carl Spitz, who so arduously serves in training hundreds of dogs for patrol duty. The war dogs you will see in this picture were delivered to the Army immediately after the scenes were photographed. They are now doing their part—with you—in our Country's . . . . MARCH TO VICTORY!*

Billy Freeman (Billy Lee) lives with his dog, Pal (Ace), and his ex-Marine father, Captain Freeman (Addison Richards), a hero of World War I. Freeman has been rejected for service this time around, since he is unable to pass the physical. Depressed and unemployed, Freeman has become an alcoholic. Pal saves the day when Billy sends him to Dogs for Defense and Freeman is heartened that one member of the family is still able to serve their country. A large part of the movie is taken up by demonstrating the war dogs' training with the use of narration, much like a Disney Real Life Adventure film. The narrator explains that the dogs are confused, but a "kindly" trainer will teach them all they need to know to be great patrol dogs.

War Dogs, originally titled *Unsung Heroes* before its release, is one of many examples of German Shepherd movie stars being used in propaganda. While *War Dogs* encourages families to donate their house pets to Dogs for Defense, Rin-Tin-Tin was once a supporter of America First and its fight against the United States joining the World Court. A pamphlet written in the first person from Rin-Tin-Tin's perspective told how the "World Famous Dog Actor" had been found by Lee Duncan amid the horrors of war: "And I don't want to live to see it again."

My Pal, Wolf (1944)

GSD: Grey Shadow as *Wolf*
Trainer: Frank V. Barnes
Director: Alfred L. Werker
Costars: Sharyn Moffet, Jill Esmond
Country: USA
Status: Rare

The child star of *My Pal, Wolf*, Sharyn Moffet, was seven years old when she appeared alongside Grey Shadow in what was his last major film role and one of her first. The story shows characters that are overstated to the point of being caricatures, yet framing that little girl next to the enormous sable Shepherd cannot help but be adorable. In one scene, Grey Shadow picks up a cardboard box, carries it to the girl, climbs inside, and curls up in the laughably small space. This kind of extreme cuteness could only work in a girl-and-her-dog movie.

Wolf (Grey Shadow) is not seen until twenty minutes into the film as the first part is dedicated to the little girl, Gretchen (Sharyn Moffet), living in a large country house and taken care of by servants rather than her working parents. Her new governess, Miss Munn (Jill Esmond) arrives at the house and tells Gretchen she will not tolerate lies from the child. She refuses to believe Gretchen's story of a wolf in a cave that she has been feeding. It turns out the wolf is a German Shepherd who has been trapped in a partially boarded-up well. Much to Munn's annoyance, Gretchen's father (Bruce Edwards) gives her permission to keep him. But Munn uncovers Wolf's Army collar and calls to report the AWOL dog. Gretchen is devastated and eventually takes her case to the Secretary of War (Edward Fielding) to plead for her dog. There, he explains to her what war dogs mean to the country and that Wolf really belongs to the whole United States.

Just as blatant as *War Dogs* (see previous entry) though using a different angle, *My Pal, Wolf* is another example of a World War II propaganda film. If it wasn't so improbable, the story is actually entertaining, and it is certainly refreshing to see a girl-and-dog film among the dozens of boy-and-dog films. *The New York Times* review said that Hollywood could not get enough of bringing the war home through movies and that *My Pal, Wolf* took this idea to new heights by bringing the war "right into the nursery."

Adventures of Rusty (1945)

GSD: Ace as *Rusty*
Trainer: Earl Johnson
Director: Paul Burnford
Costars: Ted Donaldson, Margaret Lindsay
Country: USA
Status: Limited availability

The *Rusty* series of films began with this one and went on for seven sequels, though Ace starred in only the first one. For the rest of the series, Flame, another handsome dog, filled the part of Rusty, playing opposite child star Ted Donaldson in each. In 1998, Columbia released three of the *Rusty* films on VHS, but they have otherwise never been commercially available. You can catch most of the films occasionally on the Turner Classic Movie Channel. The whole series is: *Adventures of Rusty* (1945), *The Return of Rusty* (1946), *For the Love of Rusty* (1947), *The Son of Rusty* (1947), *My Dog Rusty* (1948), *Rusty Leads the Way* (see page 68), *Rusty Saves a Life* (1949), and *Rusty's Birthday* (1949).

Danny (Ted Donaldson) is having a bad day when his father (Conrad Nagel) marries Ann (Margaret Lindsay) and his dog, terrier-mix Skippy, is hit by a truck and killed. When he finds the neighbor's vicious ex-Nazi German Shepherd, Rusty (Ace), wandering alone, Danny takes the dog home and hides him in the cellar. Danny tries to communicate with the help of his father's old German dictionary, but the dog remains aloof. After Danny's father and stepmother find out about Rusty, Danny has to go back to his neighbor and confess that he has the dog, but the neighbor is happy to see the back of him and tells Danny to keep him. Danny's angry attitude toward his new stepmother is mirrored by Rusty's attitude toward Danny, and first Danny and Rusty, then Ann, go to see a psychiatrist, looking for solutions.

Although positive reinforcement methods of training, such as the No Change Response System used by SeaWorld trainers, are often thought of as new and modern, the techniques described to Danny by the psychiatrist to tame his savage dog in 1945 are the same as those techniques today: reinforcing all desired behaviors with praise, affection, and food while ignoring all unwanted behaviors.

One-sheet poster from *Danny Boy*, featuring a painting of Ace. (Author's collection)

Danny Boy (1946)

GSD: Ace as *Danny Boy*
Trainer: Earl Johnson
Director: Terry Morse
Costars: Robert "Buzz" Henry, Ralph Lewis
Country: USA
Status: Available on DVD

"Marine Hero of the K-9 Corps Comes Home!" claims the movie poster for *Danny Boy*, along with the politically incorrect tag, "The Devil Dog Jap Killer!" This U.S. Marine Corps devil dog was played by Ace in his second to last film. The last, *God's Country* (1946), was released a few months later.

Danny Boy (Ace) arrives home after a two-year tour of duty in the South Pacific during World War II. Danny Boy's homecoming is celebrated by Jimmy Bailey (Robert Henry) and his young friends, but Jimmy soon becomes concerned that the dog, now a decorated war hero, no longer recognizes him. After walking Danny Boy home from the train station, Jimmy tells his mother (Helen Brown) that they sent him the wrong dog. She proves it is Danny Boy by finding an old scar. Slowly, with the help of Danny Boy's Marine friend, Joe Cameron (Ralph Lewis), Jimmy begins reintroducing the dog to civilian life. But evil neighbor "Grumpy" Andrews (Walter Soderling) is spreading the rumor that the ex-war dog is vicious. He steals Danny Boy, but the dog escapes his captors to make his way home. When Danny Boy tries to settle the score, he finds himself in court, with Jimmy pleading for his life.

Danny Boy was once released on TV as a 26-minute short entitled *The Adventures of Danny Boy* (also *Danny Boy: A Boy and His Dog*). Though less edited than that, the DVD release of the film in 2007 by a company called Reel Enterprises has nine minutes cut out of the middle (when Danny Boy is being stolen). Reel Enterprises' DVDs are of horrible quality to begin with, but the abrupt cut, and large amount of missing footage make it well worth trying to find this film from a different source.

My Dog Shep (1946)

GSD: Flame as *Shep*
Trainer: Frank V. Barnes
Director: Ford Beebe
Costars: Tom Neal, William Farnum
Country: USA
Status: Available on DVD

As Ace entered his retirement years, a new dog came on the scene with just as handsome a face and as much screen presence as the older Ace, but a very different personality. While Ace stood as if carved from marble while his child costars fawned over him in films like *Danny Boy* (see previous entry), Flame would wag his tail and play fetch. And where Ace seemed always to be on high alert, watching his trainer for the next cue, Flame appears better able to relax.

Dannie Barker (Lanny Rees) finds a beautiful German Shepherd Dog (Flame) abandoned at a gas station on his way to live at his aunt and uncle's farmhouse after his parents were killed in a car accident. His cruel uncle and bratty cousin make life miserable and Dannie hides the dog, whom he names Shep, in a haystack. After Uncle Matt (Russell Simpson) chases the dog from the property with a rifle, Dannie runs away after him. The two wander alone until they meet Carter Latham (William Farnum), an old man who is feeling equally unloved after his son and daughter-in-law have planned to send him away to an old folks' home. Latham, Dannie, and Shep form a close friendship, but their pleasant stint as tramps is short-lived: Dannie is being hunted down with a reward on his head after his uncle finds out that his parents left him a $100,000 inheritance. Then Dannie's new friend, Lorna (Janet Chapman), is kidnapped. Dannie rushes to help her and is taken along as well. It's up to Shep to save them.

The majority of Flame's career was made up of boy-and-his-dog films. He played the recurring role of Rusty in that series, Shep in this one, and Pal in a series of short films spinning off from the 1948 feature *Night Wind*. Flame and child star Gary Gray, who starred in *The Painted Hills* (1951) with Lassie, featured in most of the Pal films. Gray, who worked with Lassie both in film and on stage, remembered Flame as "The smartest dog I ever worked with." *My Dog Shep* was Flame's second film after *The Return of Rusty*.

Rin Tin Tin III smiles for the camera with Lee Duncan's daughter, Virginia. (Author's collection)

The Return of Rin Tin Tin (1947)

GSD: Rin Tin Tin III as himself (just *Rin Tin Tin*)

Trainer: Lee Duncan

Director: Max Nosseck

Costars: Robert Blake, Donald Woods

Country: USA

Status: Available on DVD

Throughout World War II, Lee Duncan's dogs made few film appearances. Duncan, like another famed Hollywood

trainer, Carl Spitz, had begun channeling his skills into helping the U.S. military meet its huge demand for trained war
dogs. Duncan trained an estimated 5,000 dogs for the K-9
Corps, as well as instructing others how to train and handle
the dogs.

Rin Tin Tin III, the son of Rin Tin Tin Jr. and
Treulene, and grandson of Rin-Tin-Tin and Nanette, plays a
prized German Shepherd who runs away from his angry
owner and finds a traumatized orphan named Paul (Robert
Blake) living in a monastery. Paul is afraid of the dog, but
kind Father Matthew (Donald Woods) encourages him to
make friends and tells him they can keep Rin Tin Tin as long
as no one claims him. Paul does befriend the dog. Their
bond draws him out of his frightened shell before Rin Tin
Tin's owner, Gordon Melrose (Steve Pendleton), arrives to
take the dog away. Rin Tin Tin will not be separated from
the boy, however, and breaks out of his kennel repeatedly to
return to Paul. In a sense, *The Return of Rin Tin Tin* was an
early animal-assisted therapy film, showing how positive an
impact a dog's companionship can have on stressed children.

The Return of Rin Tin Tin is one of those unfortunate
films that has been widely released on DVD without ever
receiving a proper transfer or restoration. Although filmed in
color, at a cost of $250,000, the existing prints are so dam-
aged that the film appears mostly to be sepia. So impressed
with the dog was producer William Stephens that he
optioned rights to produce a series of films starring Rin Tin

Tin III for Romay Pictures, Inc.—but it was not to be. The company went under, and it was not until the 1950s TV show *The Adventures of Rin Tin Tin* that Rin Tin Tin was again seen on the screen.

Rusty Leads the Way (1948)

GSD: Flame as *Rusty*

Trainer: Frank V. Barnes

Director: Will Jason

Costars: Ted Donaldson, Sharyn Moffett

Country: USA

Status: Rare

Child star Ted Donaldson does a lot of growing throughout the *Rusty* series, which was made over four years. Fifteen years old, but playing thirteen in this, the sixth *Rusty* film, Donaldson enjoyed working with his outgoing costar. In his interview for *Growing Up on the Set*, he remembered Flame as being very intelligent and affectionate and says he was "a sweetheart of a dog." Another child actor, Jimmy Hunt, who appeared in *Rusty's Birthday*, received one of Flame's puppies as a gift. Frank Barnes seems to have enjoyed being able to offer pups to children he worked with on sets; he did the same with Grey Shadow's puppies.

Half-sheet poster from *Rusty Leads the Way.* (Author's collection)

Rusty Leads the Way was the first feature film to show what guide dog training was like and help increase public awareness about these dogs. Danny (Ted Donaldson) and Rusty (Flame) meet a new neighbor, Penny (Sharyn Moffett), and are soon caught up in the town school board's case to send her to the state school for the blind. Wishing Penny could go to the local school, Danny proposes that she get a guide dog. Penny, who is afraid of failure, resists the idea. When Penny does at last agree to try working with a guide dog, she dislikes the Boxer, Tubby, at the school, resenting him for being more affectionate with his trainer, Ms. Adams (Paula Raymond), than her. After she panics during a street-crossing test, Penny wants nothing more to do with Tubby, although Tubby and Rusty have other ideas.

Before production began, Sharyn Moffett spent days learning to work with her Boxer guide at Guide Dogs for the Blind in San Rafael, California. The scenes in the film of Penny's training with Tubby were filmed at the school, and its trainers provided the technical advice for the production. Guide Dogs for the Blind was the first guide dog school on the West Coast, founded by Lois Merrihew and Don Donaldson in 1942. The first guide dogs trained through the school were three female German Shepherds: Lady, Vicki, and Blondie.

The Big Cat (1949)

GSD: Zoro as *Spike*
Trainer: Unknown
Director: Phil Karlson
Costars: Lon McCallister, Peggy Ann Garner
Country: USA
Status: Available on DVD

The GSD in this film belongs to the bad guy, which is most unusual. Zoro, whose name was sometimes spelled *Zorro*, holds an important place in this cat movie. A huge, white German Shepherd with a very broad chest, Zoro appeared in a small number of wilderness films beginning right before the much better known Chinook started his career.

A young man from Philadelphia named Danny (Lon McCallister) goes to the wilderness in search of work from an old friend of his deceased mother. He finds Tom (Preston Foster) is none too receptive to the idea, since his own business ran out of money and there's a terrible draught going on. If only he could kill the local outlaw cougar for money, he might be able to employ Danny. An angry neighbor, Gil (Forrest Tucker), complicates things even more for Danny. After attempts to hunt the cat end in disaster, Danny sets out to find it alone, or almost alone. Spike (Zoro), Gil's German Shepherd, goes with him. The dog tracks the cougar, corners it, and saves Danny's life, proving that you should never leave home without a good GSD.

It was publicized that the fight between Zoro and the mountain lion was unplanned: "One of the most thrilling fight scenes in motion picture history was enacted on location . . . and it was purely accidental!" This propaganda goes on to say Zoro saw the cougar on set and broke free of his leash to attack it. The crew then spent five minutes trying to separate the two animals and both were injured. In the meantime, the fight was captured on film. The most obvious flaw in this explanation of the scene is that if animal trainers and crew members were frantically trying to separate the animals, they would have been visible on camera. It is clear from watching the film, with the fight in the cave and the dog rescuing Danny, that the combat was scripted, but the surprise fight made a better story.

Kazan (1949)

GSD: Zoro as *Kazan*
Trainer: Unknown
Director: Will Jason
Costars: Stephen Dunne, Lois Maxwell
Country: USA
Status: Rare

"James Oliver Curwood's Great Dog Adventure!" according to lobby cards, *Kazan* was yet another adaptation of the famed adventure author's fiction. Curwood, who was born in Owosso, Michigan, in 1878 and published his first novel in 1908, provided the source material for more GSD films from the 1920s through the 1950s than any other writer—over thirty—though his dog novels did not really feature GSDs, but rather spitz-type dogs, wolf crosses, or pure wolves. One of Curwood's novels was even adapted into the film that featured Rin-Tin-Tin's first movie performance: *The Man from Hell's River* (1922). His works continued to be adapted into GSD films as recently as the 1990s, though possibly his best known novel-to-film was not a dog movie at all, but *The Bear* (1988).

Zoro with Stephen Dunne and Lois Maxwell on a *Kazan* lobby card. (Author's collection)

Zoro stars in this sad story of a dog who loses his master in an avalanche, is mistaken for a wolf and shot at, finds a wolf mate who is killed by a cougar, then is trapped, abused, and thrown into an illegal dogfighting ring. The plot of *Kazan* is fraught with more setbacks than many suspense films. The story unfolds as several people, including conservationist Thomas Weyman (Stephen Dunne) and Louise Maitlin (Lois Maxwell), recall meeting Kazan (Zoro) at different points in his life. When everyone gathers for the big dogfight, they find Kazan and his opponent, a Great Dane, will not fight each other. Villain Sandz Jepson (Joe Sawyer) falls into the ring while trying to escape the irate crowd, and Kazan turns on the man, but Maitlin comes to his rescue.

The first film adaptation of *Kazan* was made in 1921, though its sequel, *Baree, Son of Kazan*, had already been adapted in 1918, only a year after it was published. The book, *Kazan: Wolf-Dog of the North*, was first published in 1914. Both films have been remade multiple times since then. Most starred German Shepherds.

Shep Comes Home (1949)

GSD: Flame as *Shep*
Trainer: Frank V. Barnes
Director: Ford Beebe
Costars: Billy Kimbley, Martin Garralaga
Country: USA
Status: Limited availability

Flame appeared in few films that were not about a boy and his dog. Although he had diversity in training and the abilities to pull off just about any role, he never appeared as a war dog on the front lines, a crime-fighting K-9, or, thankfully, a companion to trappers or Mounties. The closest he came to the latter was appearing in a single western, *Northwest Stampede*, in 1948, a year in which he starred in no less than seven films. One of his last films was also his most unique: *You Never Can Tell* (1951), in which Flame plays King, who inherits millions of dollars from his master, is killed, and then is reincarnated as a man (Dick Powell) to solve his own murder case.

Shep Comes Home illustrates a dramatic increase in the quality of dog screenplays versus ten years before. The characters are not recurring in the *Shep* films, as they are in the *Rusty* series. Only Flame playing the dog named Shep remains the same. An orphan is again included, since, for reasons best known to writers, all dog films need an orphan, or at least one dead parent—usually the mother. Orphan Larry (Billy Kimbley) runs away with Shep when he finds out that he will be sent to an orphanage without his dog. The pair get caught up with a likable drifter, Manuel Ortiz (Martin Garralaga), and two bank robbers who frame Ortiz with the shooting of a sheriff. Oritz is arrested and Larry is left with the crooks. It's up to Shep to bring the men to justice. Michael Whalen, who worked with Lightning in *White Fang* (see page 41) and Grey Shadow in *Sign of the Wolf* (see page 54), plays one of the bad guys.

Flame's huge vocabulary included knowing the difference between "Look left," "Look right," "Look stage left," and "Look stage right." He even won two PATSY Awards— once presented to animal actors and their trainers by the AHA. His desire to work, agreeable temperament, amiability with children, and intelligence—not to mention his good looks—were all passed down to his son: the dog who, in a few more years, children across the country would recognize by the cry, "Yo, Rinty!"

Flame, star of the *Rusty* and *Shep* series, with Ted Donaldson in 1949. (Author's collection)

Super Dogs: The 1950s

While Rin Tin Tin and Lassie were performing amazing feats of bravery and super-intelligence on TV, a dog known as Chinook was getting his name in huge letters on movie posters beside the starring humans. Dogs were still in press material, still incredible. From the feature film premiere of Roy Rogers's Bullet to Dorothy Crider's famous White Shadow German Shepherds to London's astounding performance in *The Littlest Hobo*, the 1950s were, in many ways, the last hurrah of the "Wonder Dogs."

Spoilers of the Plains (1951)

GSD: Ace as *Bullet*

Trainer: Earl Johnson

Director: William Witney

Costars: Roy Rogers, Penny Edwards

Country: USA

Status: Available on DVD

Many people are familiar with Roy Rogers's famous horse, Trigger, and his German Shepherd, Bullet, from the *Roy Rogers Show*, which aired on TV during the 1950s. Before the show, however, Bullet appeared alongside Rogers and Trigger in some of their feature films, the first of which was *Spoilers of the Plains*. In this film, Bullet is played by Ace, though not Earl Johnson's original Ace, whose last film was in 1946. This Bullet was probably really Ace Jr., one of Ace's sons, who appeared in a few films before his untimely death in an accident.

Spoilers of the Plains takes a departure from typical Roy Rogers cowboy plots. It has Rogers mixed up with scientists setting off rockets on his home turf and bad guys trying to steal valuable rocket technology. There's still plenty of horseback riding and occasional singing to keep the story in line with the typical scripts used by the "King of Cowboys." Bullet (Ace) is introduced without ceremony at the beginning of the film. The dog more than proves his worth as he saves Rogers's life multiple times, fighting off a Doberman Pinscher belonging to the rocket thieves, sensing an ambush, and pointing out a bomb to Rogers in time for the latter to get it out of the scientists' camp.

Roy Rogers kept German Shepherd Dogs at his home ranch and had multiple dogs named Bullet in real life. But the dogs who appeared in the films and show were not his own. The dogs playing Bullet were owned and trained by Earl Johnson for some years before William Koehler—famed trainer for Walt Disney, among others—took over. Toward the end of the TV series, Frank Inn, trainer of Benji, also supplied Bullets. Besides the numerous actor dogs who represented Bullet, stunt doubles who were trained attack dogs were imported from Germany so the main dog did not have to do any bite work.

Northwest Territory (1951)

GSD: Harvey as *Chinook*
Trainer: Dorothy Crider
Director: Frank McDonald
Costars: Kirby Grant, Gloria Saunders
Country: USA
Status: Rare

The son of Earl Johnson's Ace, Harvey Brindlesiff Offner, the most famous white German Shepherd film star in history, was not really white. Harvey, who was commonly referred to as Chinook, or Chinook I, both on and off screen, was a silver dog with some dark highlights. It was the black and white cameras of the time that made Chinook, Kirby Grant's famous companion in a series of wilderness films, look so white. The ten films of the series were based on James Oliver Curwood stories.

This sixth film in Chinook and Grant's Royal Canadian Mounted Police saga has Chinook and Corporal Rod Webb (Grant) trying to solve a murder—or Webb is trying to solve it. Chinook already knows what's going on. The story features a rough bad guy duo, a beautiful young woman, and even an orphaned boy. A piece of cloth Chinook has torn from a Mackinaw belonging to one of the killers is all Webb has to go on in the case—until the dog attacks a man at a trading post for no apparent reason.

Harvey belonged to actress Dorothy Crider and was trained by her, as well as Sam Williamson, who assisted training on some of the *Lassie* TV episodes of the 1950s. Crider founded a kennel, White Shadow Ranch, where she bred large, beautiful, and intelligent white German Shepherds. Harvey, who appeared in over 180 films and shows, both on television and in live performances, was not her only star Shepherd: his son, White Shadow Crider, played White Shadow in the Walt Disney Mickey Mouse Club TV serial, *Corky and White Shadow* (1955–1956). White Shadow was in almost as many films and shows as his father and won three PATSY Awards. Tango of White Shadow, Crider's third-generation star, appeared as Bullet in live performances with Roy Rogers and won two PATSYs for films.

Fangs of the Arctic (1953)

GSD: Harvey as *Chinook*
Trainer: Dorothy Crider
Director: Rex Bailey
Costars: Kirby Grant, Lorna Hanson
Country: USA
Status: Rare

As popular as he was with audiences, Harvey had a bad reputation on set. After he bit numerous members of the cast and crew while working on the Mountie series, the nearly 140-pound Shepherd was kept muzzled while not in front of the cameras. Although Grant got along with Harvey, many others were justifiably leery of the temperamental star, who did not always listen to his mistress. Harvey was so aggressive toward *Fangs of the Arctic* bad guy Warren Douglas that the actor avoided him on the set at all times unless they had a scene together.

Corporal Rod Webb (Kirby Grant), with Chinook and Constable Mike Kelly (Robert Sherman), is once again on the trail of a murderer. Posing as trappers, Webb and Kelly are soon involved with a gang of men trapping beaver illegally. Kelly meets boyhood sweetheart Sandra Dubois (Lorna Hanson) before his own unfortunate demise, leaving Webb and Chinook another case to handle. The murderers and trappers are traced back to a single gang headed by Matt Oliver (Douglas), a supposed mining engineer, and Chinook finally has his moment to go after the actor.

Dorothy Crider was devoted to her dogs and to her breeding goals for healthy white Shepherds with great intelligence. Harvey was even best man at her wedding. Crider was an outspoken advocate against the discrimination of white German Shepherd Dogs have faced in conformation show rings. After working with light and dark German Shepherds for nearly thirty years, she concluded that there was no difference between dogs of varied colors: "The difference lies in the individual animal, not the coat color." Crider ran a newspaper ad promoting her white dogs at stud: "Proven sires of show, pets, size, beauty and actors." The Chinook White Shadow line continues today.

One-sheet poster from *Fangs of the Arctic*. (Author's collection)

Police Dog (1955)

GSD: Rex III as himself
Trainer: Arthur Holman
Director: Derek Twist
Costars: Tim Turner, Joan Rice
Country: UK
Status: Limited availability

A handsome, plush-coated, black and tan GSD, Rex III was England's, and possibly the world's, most famous police dog in the 1950s. The first dog trained to detect drugs, Rex was credited with 125 arrests in his six-year career. Born on March 11, 1949, Rex met his handler, Arthur Holman, in March 1950. He got his name from being the third Rex to serve in the police force and also happened to be the third dog named Rex owned by Holman. Rex learned to obey only Holman and take food only from him, though he had one quirk to his obedience: he refused to heel on lead and would only ever heel when his leash was removed.

In 1954, at the height of his career, when Rex's fame had spread as England's top police dog, Holman was approached by producer Harold Huth and director Derek Twist. They were making a film about a police dog and wanted to use the real thing. And Rex was the very best. Holman was initially eager to work with his famed dog on a movie but soon found the ten-hour-days, cold nights, and hot studio lights for six weeks straight were not what they were cracked up to be. Scenes in which the dog was being fed by an actor had to be shot without sound and the dialogue dubbed in so Holman could constantly be telling Rex it was okay to take the food. On the other hand, Rex climbed a ladder so fast and easily that the director called for take after take in order to get a shot that made the climb appear arduous for him.

The story centers around policeman Frank Mason (Tim Turner) and his training and work with Rex after Mason's partner is shot while on patrol. Mason is thirsting for revenge and hopes Rex will be the one who can catch the killer. He has to first convince both his boss and his girlfriend, Pat Lewis (Joan Rice), that keeping the dog is a good idea. At first, Lewis is thrilled by the dog, but gradually, she becomes jealous of Mason's attention to him. In the end, Rex proves his worth, saving Mason from the same villain who shot his partner.

Another plush-/long-coated GSD appeared in the UK production of *The Bridal Path* in 1959. In the film, Bluey plays a police dog named Rex who is sent to stop a man on the run but instead joins him in a dingy and travels home with him.

How Wong Fei Hung Vanquished the Ferocious Dog in Shamian (1956)

Also known as *Huang Fei-hong Shamian fu shen quan*
GSD: Mr. Lucky as the ferocious dog
Trainer: Unknown
Director: Wang Tianlin
Costars: Kwan Tak Hing, Tso Tat-wah
Country: China
Status: Unknown

Wong Fei Hung was an actual man who became a Chinese folk hero. The celebrated traditional doctor and martial artist was portrayed in so many films and shows from the 1940s to the 2000s that he earned the distinction of becoming the most portrayed character ever on film. The Wong Fei Hung movies starring Kwan Tak Hing included ninety-nine feature films which follow the hero through feats of skill and bravery as he does things implied by very literal titles, such as *Wong Fei Hung Rescues the Fishmonger* (1956) and *How Wong Fei Hung Pitted 7 Lions Against the Dragon* (1956). *How Wong Fei Hung Vanquished the Ferocious Dog in Shamian* goes by multiple titles, including the original, above, and a variant English translation, *How Huang Fei-hong Vanquished the Terrible Hound at Shamian*.

The ferocious dog is played by Mr. Lucky, a sable German Shepherd, who is sent to attack the medical office of Wong Fei Hung (Kwan Tak Hing) by his villainous master.

Wong fights back against the dog, who leaps over his shoulder and performs other canine kung-fu moves before Wong defeats him. He then goes after the dog's owner with some human martial arts. In the end, Wong forces the instigator of the trouble, the man behind both the dog and his owner, to donate his riches to charity.

Wong Fei Hung has since been portrayed by both Jackie Chan and Jet Li, making him better known to American audiences. But the old films are extremely difficult to come by and the current whereabouts of any print of *Ferocious Dog* are uncertain. Mr. Lucky was not alone as a German Shepherd performer in 1950s Chinese film. Other old features in the genre include *The Dogs Save the Day* (1953), about police dogs, and *The Valiant Dog Saves Its Master* (1953), about dogs rescuing their mistresses from kidnappers. The latter starred two German Shepherds: Mr. Sing Hoi and Miss Ai Luck.

The Brain from the Planet Arous (1957)

GSD: *George*
Trainer: Dorothy Crider (unconfirmed)
Director: Nathan H. Juran
Costars: John Agar, Joyce Meadows
Country: USA
Status: Available on DVD

Without firm evidence that George was one of Dorothy Crider's White Shadow German Shepherd Dogs, it would be wrong to say that Crider was without a doubt the trainer. However, the dog in *The Brain from the Planet Arous* is indistinguishable from Crider's dogs, both in physical appearance and temperament. George is most likely played by Tango.

It's a case of "good brain/bad brain" when an escaped alien criminal, Gor, lands on Earth and is tracked down by the law; alien good guy, Val. Why the aliens take the form of enormous, floating human brains with huge, glowing eyes is never explained—or even remarked upon by the humans who encounter them. But as with most such drive-in films, it really doesn't need to be. The white German Shepherd, George, belongs to Sally Fallon (Joyce Meadows), who is engaged to Steve March (John Agar). But March is attacked by Gor, who inhabits him and takes control of his mind and body. Val makes friendly contact with Fallon and uses George's body to shadow Gor in an effort to bring him to justice. Though he does not receive a large amount of screen time, George plays an important role as he protects Fallon and helps Val with his mission.

Prolific actor John Agar appeared in around one hundred films and TV shows during his career—mostly B western and sci-fi features like *The Brain from the Planet Arous*. Another of his films with a white German Shepherd was *Attack of the Puppet People* (1958), although the dog's role in the case of that film was very minimal. Agar was much better known for his marriage to Shirley Temple in 1945 and subsequent divorce four years later than for his work with costarring dogs.

The Courage of Rin Tin Tin (1957)

GSD: J.R. as *Rin Tin Tin*
Trainer: Frank V. Barnes
Director: Robert G. Walker
Costars: Lee Aaker, James Brown
Country: USA
Status: Limited availability

The Courage of Rin Tin Tin, sometimes called *The Challenge of Rin Tin Tin*, was one of two movie spinoffs that came out of the TV series *The Adventures of Rin Tin Tin*, which aired 166 episodes from 1954 to 1959. Child star Lee Aaker narrowly missed out on being cast as Timmy in *Lassie*, only to get the role of Rusty six months later. The canine star of the show and films was named J.R.—short for Junior—and was the son of Flame, not a Rin-Tin-Tin descendent. Lee Duncan was originally offered the job as head trainer for the show. Duncan, who by then was in his sixties, declined, although Rin Tin Tin IV, trained by Duncan, did appear in *The Adventures of Rin Tin Tin* as J.R.'s double.

The show followed the exploits of an orphaned boy and his dog who were taken in and looked after by soldiers of the 101st Cavalry in the 1800s. In the film, Rusty (Lee Aaker) and Rin Tin Tin (J.R.) must face first a killer mountain lion, then a pack of diabolical wolves, as the two head north with Lieutenant "Rip" Masters (James Brown) to assist in dealings with natives by the Royal Canadian Mounted Police. "Rinty" thwarts the White Wolf, only to take over his pack and lead it away from Rusty in order to save his young master. While he's away, Rinty provides some spiritual intervention to assist a native chief and then save his life.

The wolf pack in *The Courage of Rin Tin Tin* is played mostly by Siberian Huskies, but the White Wolf is played by a few different dogs, one of which appears to be Zoro, star of *Kazan* (see page 72). The show sparked hundreds of tie-in items, from comic books to board games to Halloween costumes. Today, TV's Rinty is what most people think of when they hear the name Rin Tin Tin. The show, not the original star, is largely what has kept the memory of the name alive.

Kelly and Me (1957)

GSD: *Kelly*

Trainer: Unknown

Director: Robert Z. Leonard

Costars: Van Johnson, Piper Laurie

Country: USA

Status: Rare

Kelly and Me is a fascinating movie, featuring one of the most extraordinary and memorable canine performances you will ever see. The white German Shepherd star, Kelly, does everything from song and dance numbers to attack scenes in the film and won a PATSY Award for his performance. While many of his actions, such as walking backward on his hind legs across a stage, are no different than those of other "trick" dogs, the often very wide angles and limited cuts throughout the film make Kelly a standout. Van Johnson had recently terminated an exclusive contract with MGM before starting production on *Kelly and Me* in early 1956.

Set in 1930, the story centers around Len Carmody (Van Johnson), a washed-up Vaudeville performer, and the Vaudeville trick dog Kelly, whom Carmody accidentally befriends by feeding him peanuts. When Kelly's angry trainer takes his other dogs and moves on without Kelly, the Shepherd adopts Carmody and saves his failing routine. After Mina Van Runkel (Piper Laurie), the daughter of eminent movie producer Walter Van Runkel (Onslow Stevens), runs into Carmody and Kelly on a train, she hurries to tell her father about the extraordinarily talented dog. Van Runkel wants Kelly for a film, but Carmody insists on getting the starring role for himself before he will agree to sign Kelly on. What follows is Kelly's rise to the top with his likable but bumbling handler in tow.

The films Kelly does within *Kelly and Me* include all of the popular themes of the time such as Yukon, Mountie, and World War I stories. There's also a nod to the current (in 1957) *Rin Tin Tin* TV show when Kelly appears in a U.S. Cavalry drama. Prop issues of *Variety* in the film said that Kelly was the "biggest thing since sound." Filmed in color, *Kelly and Me* was theatrically released by Universal and has never been released on VHS or DVD.

London on a lobby card for *The Littlest Hobo*, with Buddy Hart and Wendy Stuart. (Author's collection)

The Littlest Hobo (1958)

GSD: London as *Hobo*
Trainer: Charles P. Eisenmann
Director: Charles R. Rondeau
Costars: Buddy Hart, Wendy Stuart
Country: USA
Status: Rare

Charles Eisenmann was a pitcher for the Chicago White Sox when a war injury to his elbow cost him his job. He went home to Los Angeles, where he began spending all his time with a nine-month-old German Shepherd puppy, London. When Eisenmann got a new contract, London went with him to play for the Kearney, Nebraska, Irishmen. London impressed the team by choosing a 35-inch Jackie Robinson bat out of a huge selection after Eisenmann had not touched it himself. London helped with warmups and pepper games, soon drawing big crowds and making guest appearances all over the region. One woman who saw the dog perform wrote in to the TV show *You Asked for It*. Soon, Eisenmann and London were on their way to Hollywood.

London was offered his own television show, but the producers were so delighted with the dog, they made a feature film instead. The film, originally titled *The Miracle of the Lamb*, centers around a pet lamb being rescued from a slaughterhouse by London. During the first scene that was filmed, London performed a complex array of running, jumping, stopping, and looking feats, all in a rundown shipyard. Then he returned to his starting point to fetch the lamb by a short piece of rope around its neck. London performed everything asked of him the first time in one flawless run without stops. Then the director told Eisenmann that they were ready to shoot the first take—the camera had not been rolling.

In the film, which was retitled *The Littlest Hobo*, London plays a wandering hobo who finds a boy, Tommy (Buddy Hart), grieving for the loss of his pet lamb. London saves the lamb from slaughter, only to find police on their trail, as well as a group of tramps who want a mutton dinner. Eisenmann plays a tramp and can be seen on one of the lobby cards for the film depicting his scene. London eventually leads his charge to the governor's house, where he manages to convince wheelchair-bound Molly (Wendy Stuart) that she can stand again. She adopts the lamb, with Tommy's approval, but London is soon off again, still a hobo.

Wolf Dog (1958)

GSD: Prince as *Dog*

Trainer: Unknown

Director: Sam Nefield

Costars: Jim Davis, Allison Hayes

Countries: Canada, USA

Status: Rare (see description)

The hero of *Wolf Dog* was a black and tan German Shepherd Dog named Prince who already had some star qualities when he landed the movie deal. Prince was the great-great-great-grandson of Rin-Tin-Tin, though he did not belong to Lee Duncan. He was a seven-year-old working dog with the Royal Canadian Mounted Police in Bolton, Ontario, Canada, when Sam Nefield, the director, chose him for the role. After filming, he returned to his day job.

Jim Hughes (Jim Davis) moves to a farm with his wife, Ellen (Allison Hayes), and son, Paul (Tony Brown). When Jim refuses to sell his land to his new neighbor, Clem Krivak (Austin Willis), the man threatens to reveal what he knows about Jim's past as a convict, then sends his dog after Paul's dog, killing it. Paul finds an abandoned wolf pup in a storm and pleads with his father to let him keep it. Dog (Prince) grows and proves himself when he tracks down cattle rustlers organized by Clem, then saves Paul from drowning in a river. Clem tries turning his own dog on Dog, but this time, the villain is on the losing end of the fight. Clem comes looking for Dog with a rifle, but Jim intervenes.

After its July 1958 release, *Wolf Dog* apparently vanished from the face of the Earth—that is, until Jeff Wilson started trying to uncover it from its movie netherworld and return it to the screen for those who still remembered the filming in Markdale, Ontario, Canada. Many years later, Wilson got his wish; *Wolf Dog*, of which there is a complete surviving copy at the U.S. Library of Congress, was screened for town residents and visitors on July 6, 2007. The screenings were a huge success and a single DVD copy was also given to the Grey Highlands Municipal Library System. It can be hoped that one day *Wolf Dog* will make it onto a distributed DVD release. Until then, you can drop by the Walter Harris Memorial Library in Markdale, northwest of Toronto, to see it for yourself.

Moonwolf (1959)

Also known as *Zurück aus dem Weltall*
GSD: *Wolf*
Trainer: Unknown
Director: Georges Friedland
Costars: Carl Möhner, Anneli Sauli
Countries: Finland, West Germany
Status: Available on DVD

Filmed in Berlin, with location footage shot in Lapland, Finland, *Moonwolf* is a German language film. Dubbed for U.S. audiences, it was not released in the United States until 1966. Ten minutes were edited out of the dubbed version. The original title translates to *Back from the Universe*, and the German re-release title translates to *And the Heart Always Calls*. The English *Moonwolf* title is a reference to the space shuttle launched with the "wolf" inside by the scientists in the story. The U.S. DVD was released by Sinister Cinema under the title *Moon Wolf*.

The film is organized into sequences alternating from the present to long flashbacks. Zoologist Peter Holm (Carl Möhner) debates whether or not he is prepared to send his wolf, Wolf (a GSD), into outer space for the benefit of science and exploration, then remembers how he came to have the animal in the first place. He was studying wildlife in Lapland when he saw a wolf puppy get swept away in a river. He met the same wolf years later and realized it must be him when the woman who had him, Ara (Anneli Sauli, credited as Ann

Savo), recounted her story of rescuing him from the river as a pup. Although Dr. Holm's interest in Ara grows, he eventually returns to Germany, with the encouragement of Ara's fiancé. Wolf goes with him. After some reluctance, Dr. Holm agrees that Wolf should go up in an experimental space shuttle that will orbit the moon and return.

Moonwolf is, without a doubt, the most unique film in this book. Though the wilderness parts are old news, this is the only film in the world about a German Shepherd Dog being sent to the moon. Besides the starring German Shepherd, there are real wolves featured, as well as sled dogs including either Finnish Lapphunds or long-coated Lapinporokoiras. The fight between the Finnish dogs and wolves is disturbing and shows a wolf that is either dead or anesthetized being repeatedly bitten and shaken by a dog.

London (lower center) with four of his sons, circa 1963.
(Author's collection)

Family Friend: The 1960s

The Adventures of Rin Tin Tin had reached its finale. Flame's and Chinook's careers were over. Stars like Strongheart, Peter the Great, Flash, and Lightning were fading from public memory. As movies were becoming bigger, more expensive, and more complex, German Shepherd Dogs were disappearing from them. Police dogs, wilderness dogs, child's companions, and war dogs were still brought to the screen by talented German Shepherds in the 1960s. They could still be seen in small roles such as in *Zebra in the Kitchen* (1965), just as much as in decades past. Yet the 1960s marked a shift into the kind of dog movies we are still seeing today: family films with the dog at the center of the poster but almost never credited on it.

As they do today, reviewers might comment on a dog's ability or cuteness, but the days of being taken seriously—for one dog's performance being critiqued against another dog's—had ended. A dog was more and more becoming a prop, rather than an actor. Still, there were those dogs in the family films of the 1960s who were able to shine.

A Dog's Best Friend (1960)

GSD: *King*

Trainer: Unknown

Director: Edward L. Cahn

Costars: Bill Williams, Marcia Henderson

Country: USA

Status: Rare

A Dog's Best Friend has the distinction of having its insert poster shown on the two pages dedicated to "Dogs on Film" in the enormously popular *The Encyclopedia of the Dog*, by Bruce Fogle, D.V.M. In fact, of the six movie dog images shown in the book, half are German Shepherds, the other GSDs being London with Wendy Stuart and Rando with James Belushi.

Like those of other German Shepherd films from the 1930s through the 1960s, the advertising campaign for *A Dog's Best Friend* suggested that theater owners go to a tremendous amount of trouble to promote the film. Ideas included holding a writing contest ("I like dogs because . . .") and getting a newspaper to run photographs of local kids with their dogs and give out tickets to the show for the best photos. Other films offered ideas such as asking a boy and his German Shepherd to walk up and down outside the theater with a sign on the dog's back promoting the film, or holding a dog show for kids inside the theater lobby with movie tickets as prizes.

In *A Dog's Best Friend*, an angry, orphaned boy, Pip (Roger Mobley), gets a home with a rancher and his wife but has a hard time settling in. He finds himself involved in a crime when he meets a starving stray German Shepherd guarding a gun. Unbeknownst to Pip, the dog, King, was a former war dog whose master was recently murdered. King had attacked the killers and gotten away with the murder weapon before Pip found him. When his adoptive father, Wes Thurman (Bill Williams), discovers that Pip is taking care of the dog, Wes reports the dog to the police station, and hence to the killer: the deputy sheriff. After his accomplice confesses to the crime, both the sheriff and Wes rush to save Pip and King from the deputy, who wants the gun back and the dog dead.

One-sheet poster for *My Dog, Buddy.* (Author's collection)

My Dog, Buddy (1960)

GSD: London as *Buddy*

Trainer: Charles P. Eisenmann

Director: Ray Kellogg

Costars: Travis Lemmond, Ken Curtis

Country: USA

Status: Unknown

After the surprise success of *The Littlest Hobo* (see page 93), London got another film deal: *My Dog, Buddy*. Then in 1963, *The Littlest Hobo* was adapted as a TV show. The title role was mostly filled by four of London's sons—Thorn, Toro, Litlon, and London Jr. The Canadian series ran until 1965. In 1979, it was updated as a new show that ran until 1985, this time in color. The dog in the later shows was played by London's grandchildren and great-grandchildren.

Filmed in Dallas, *My Dog, Buddy* is the story of a boy named Ted (Travis Lemmond), who survives a car crash that kills both his parents. The only other survivor of the accident is Buddy (London), Ted's German Shepherd. When Ted is rushed from the scene by ambulance, Buddy is left behind and begins a search for his young master, vainly following every vehicle he hears with a siren. Mistaken for a missing show dog, Buddy is picked up by the police and taken to the home of Jim Foster (James H. Foster). Foster does not know the dog but takes him to the show under the pretense that Buddy is his own. Ted's doctors have also brought the unresponsive boy to the dog show in the hope that he will react to the dogs. Ted sees Buddy, but before they can be reunited, Buddy hears a siren outside and bolts for it. A chase ensues as Foster, Ted, and his doctors try to bring the pair back together.

Charles Eisenmann, with London, developed the "intellectual method" of educating a dog to understand enormous vocabularies, as opposed to training a dog with habitual commands. While working on the set of *The Littlest Hobo* TV show, Eisenmann often did not have the opportunity to see the script until the day before filming was to begin, and sometimes not until after it had already started. Such conditions would have been all but impossible for many dogs and trainers to work with, but London and family had such remarkable understanding of Eisenmann's instructions that they were able to perform flawlessly even with no prep time.

One-sheet poster for *Police Dog Story,* (Author's collection)

Police Dog Story (1961)

GSD: Rocco as *Wolf*

Director: Edward L. Cahn

Costars: James Brown, Merry Anders

Country: USA

Status: Rare

One of director Edward L. Cahn's later films, *Police Dog Story* was released a year after his earlier GSD film, *A Dog's Best Friend* (see page 101). Amazingly, it was filmed in about two weeks. It is a useful film for anyone interested in old styles of canine obstacle courses—what we would now call agility equipment—and police training methods.

A stray German Shepherd (Rocco) is adopted into a K-9 training program, but his unruly behavior lands him the name Wolf and almost costs him his new job. Much of the film is dedicated to the training of Wolf and his fellow GSD K-9s, similar to the military dog training in *War Dogs* (see page 57). Then Norm Edwards (James Brown), Wolf's handler, is sent with the dog to investigate another officer's death. He discovers a gang of arsonists who have been burning down buildings for insurance money. When the gang captures Edwards, Wolf saves him and brings the arsonists to justice, proving all those who doubted him wrong. The film resembles England's earlier *Police Dog* (see page 84).

Police Dog Story was produced during a year when Cahn directed eleven feature films—a number that would be unheard of today, and even at the time was extraordinary. Only one other was dog-related; *Boy Who Caught a Crook*, featuring a Beagle. Cahn died only two years after that, at age sixty-four. Many of Cahn's low-budget B films were later remade into some much more famous features, including *Night of the Living Dead* and *Alien*. Unfortunately, neither *Police Dog Story* nor *A Dog's Best Friend* have yet come back to the screen as new films.

The Young and the Brave (1963)

GSD: Flame as *Lobo*

Trainer: Frank V. Barnes (unconfirmed)

Director: Francis D. Lyon

Costars: Rory Calhoun, William Bendix

Country: USA

Status: Rare

The Young and the Brave is set in 1951 Korea, during the Korean War. The large, black and tan German Shepherd of the film was named Flame and resembled both the original Flame and J.R. He is possibly a descendent of theirs, though this is unconfirmed.

Seven-year-old orphan Han (Manuel Padilla) finds a G.I. war dog, Lobo (Flame), who befriends him. The two meet up with three American POW soldiers trying to make their way to friendly territory. Han's shout of "Kill, Lobo, kill!" to the huge dog when they run into the men, and Lobo's leaping for them, are priceless. The party soon joins another American on the run before one of the original number is killed by a land mine. Lobo leads the group safely though the rest of the mines and they arrive at an enemy-controlled house with a radio antenna on its roof. Though they get a message through to command, Han is separated from the rest and Lobo is injured and unable to track the boy. When the men do find the boy, Lobo saves the day once more by fighting off enemy soldiers. The film does not have a happy ending for Lobo and has only a bittersweet one for Han, illustrating the distance between new films and those of the 1930s and 1940s.

The sergeant in charge of the little group in the film is played by Rory Calhoun, an ex-con in real life who came into his acting career by accident: He was riding his horse when he met David Ladd in 1943, and Ladd's wife, agent Sue Carol Ladd, got him his first film role. He later signed with Hollywood agent Henry Willson, whose best known clients included Rock Hudson and Tab Hunter, among many others. Calhoun's birth name was Francis McCown, but Willson changed it first to Troy Donahue, then to Rory Calhoun. The actor appeared in well over one hundred different films and TV shows, including other German Shepherd movies: *Miraculous Journey* (1948, starring the original Flame) and *Won Ton Ton, the Dog Who Saved Hollywood* (see page 128).

Legend of the Northwest (1964)

Also known as *Bearheart of the Great Northwest*
GSD: *Bearheart*
Trainer: Frank V. Barnes
Director: Rand Brooks
Costars: Marshall Reed, Bill Zuckert
Country: USA
Status: Available on DVD

Legend of the Northwest was shown on television as *Bearheart of the Great Northwest*. In 2007, it was released on DVD by VCI Video as *Legend of Bearheart*. The striking black and tan dog was photographed here in color, unlike Flame. It is unfortunate that the film is so badly degraded. The dog who played Bearheart belonged to Frank Barnes. Producer/ director Rand Brooks, who knew Barnes from appearing in some *Rin Tin Tin* episodes as Corporal Randy Boone, used his own money to make *Legend of the Northwest*, and it was not even released. Not until 1978 was it seen by the public.

Mr. Adams (Marshall Reed) moves himself and his two children to a remote trading post. When he shoots a German Shepherd, mistaking it for a wolf, Abner Bassett (Denver Pyle) tells them the story of why the dog, Bearheart, has been living in the wilderness: His master was murdered and Bearheart tracked the murderer for days and nights through the forest. When at last the killer staggered into town and turned himself in, Bearheart still would not rest and eventually scared the man to death. Bassett tried to find the dog a home, but Bearheart became an outcast after a child aimed an old rifle at him in a game and the dog attacked the weapon. A long-coated GSD plays Bearheart's wolf mate.

The song "Bearheart of the Great Northwest," by Hal Hopper, heard over the opening credits, is reminiscent of songs in Walt Disney films such as *Old Yeller* (1957) and *The Legend of Lobo* (1962):

> *Bearheart of the Great Northwest, legend of the frontier trail,*
> *A gallant spirit in a giant land,*
> *A forest king on his lone outstand,*
> *Alert to the danger ever close at hand,*
> *Bearheart, Bearheart, Bearheart . . .*

Atta Girl, Kelly! (1967)

GSD: Brandy as *Kelly*
Trainer: William Koehler
Director: James Sheldon
Costars: Beau Bridges, J.D. Cannon
Country: USA
Status: Limited availability

Atta Girl, Kelly! was originally broadcast on TV in March 1967 as a three-part show from the *Wonderful World of Disney*. There were dozens of live-action Walt Disney movies starring dogs produced in the 1950s, 1960s, and 1970s, though very few with German Shepherds. Those few included *Three on the Run* (1978), in which a white German Shepherd leads a motley sled team, and *Smoke* (see page 115), both also for TV. *Atta Girl, Kelly!* was filmed partly at the campus of The Seeing Eye, Inc., in Morristown, New Jersey. It was such a hit The Seeing Eye started a Kelly fan club. In February 2009, Disney released the film for the first time ever on DVD as part of its Disney Rewards Program to help celebrate the eightieth anniversary of The Seeing Eye.

The story follows a puppy named Kelly from her earliest days of life at the Seeing Eye school. When she is old enough, Kelly is taken to her puppy raiser, Danny Richards (Billy Corcoran). She is his 4-H project for the year to come and he throws himself into the task, thrilled to have a dog. At a year old, Kelly must leave Danny and return to the school. They are both devastated by the separation, but slowly, Kelly comes to trust her new trainer, Matt Howell (Beau Bridges), who spends countless hours with her. Then it's graduation day and Kelly has to once again learn to let go and love again as she is paired with a blind partner.

There were a combination of movie dogs and guide dogs used to play the part of Kelly. The main guide dog was played by Brandy, a stunning black and silver female who later became part of the Seeing Eye's breeding program. Technical support from The Seeing Eye was provided by George Debetaz, who was vice president of training. The actor dogs playing alongside Brandy were trained by famed

Walt Disney animal trainer William Koehler, who was known for films like *Big Red* (1962), *The Incredible Journey* (1963), and *The Ugly Dachshund* (1966), as well as training Wildfire, the Bull Terrier of MGM's remarkable film, *It's a Dog's Life* (1955).

Five and the Spies (1969)

Also known as *De 5 og spionerne*

GSD: *Tim*

Trainer: Unknown

Director: Katrine Hedman

Costars: Lone Thielke, Niels Kibenich

Country: Denmark

Status: Available on DVD (PAL format only)

Five and the Spies is a Danish film based on the book *Five Go Adventuring Again*, by famed British children's author Enid Blyton. Blyton wrote a series of fifteen juvenile novels from the 1940s to the 1960s, about the Famous Five. The five are four children, Julian, Dick, Anne, Georgina ("George"), and George's dog, Timothy.

In the books, "Timmy" is a mixed breed. There have been many British productions of Blyton's *Famous Five* series, including both films and TV shows. In these, Timmy has been played by a mixed breed and a Border Collie. The two

Dutch films based on the books, the other being *De 5 i fedte-fadet*—English title *Five Get into Trouble* (1970)—are the only adaptations in which Timmy is a German Shepherd Dog.

Timmy, called only *Tim* in the film, does not always play a huge part in *Famous Five* books, though some feature him more than others. In this film adaptation, his character is central to the story. George (Lone Thielke) finds the visit of her three cousins (Niels Kibenich, Sanne Knudsen, and Mads Rahbek) overshadowed by her wicked new tutor, Mr. Roland (John Larsen). Roland takes an instant dislike to Tim. The mutual enmity increases when Tim catches Roland prowling around the house one night and Tim attacks. After the incident, George's father insists that she make Tim sleep outside at night. Tim proves himself a hero when the children get to the bottom of some strange goings-on in the house. He saves George from the bad guys, then prevents Roland's escape.

Though not extremely well known in the United States, Enid Blyton, who died in 1968, was and is one of the best-selling authors in the world. Besides dozens of film and TV adaptations like this one, her books have been translated into over ninety different languages and sold over 600 million copies worldwide. Still, Blyton's books are not without controversy: they have been widely banned in school libraries on the grounds that they are both sexist and racist.

The Comeback: The 1970s

The 1970s were a huge time for film dogs, not just Shepherds: Lassie was back on TV with a new show, Benji beat the odds to become an international superstar, and the new phenomenon of canine horror films arrived in force. In Europe, hundreds of Euro westerns were being made, and dozens featured German Shepherds as sled dogs, wolves, or the heroes of the stories. Between 1973 and 1977 alone, no less than seven adaptations of Jack London's *White Fang* were produced in Europe. Each starred a German Shepherd Dog.

The Littlest Hobo series was remade and back on television. German Shepherds even got their own Hollywood spoof with *Won Ton Ton, the Dog Who Saved Hollywood*. After a seeming decline in interest for canine film stars, the 1970s exploded with dogs on television, dogs in movies, and a whole lot of German Shepherd heroes.

Smoke (1970)

GSD: *Smoke*

Trainer: Unknown

Director: Vincent McEveety

Costars: Ron Howard, Earl Holliman

Country: USA

Status: Limited availability

Originally presented as a two-part episode on ABC's *Wonderful World of Disney*, *Smoke* aired on February 1 and 8, 1970. The first part of *Smoke* was the four hundredth episode of *The Wonderful World of Disney*. *Smoke* is based on a juvenile novel of the same name by William Corbin. The film stays much truer to the book than do most modern adaptations. Although released on VHS in 1997, *Smoke* has otherwise never been available to the public.

Fourteen-year-old Chris (Ron Howard) is having a hard time getting along with his new stepfather, Cal (Earl Holliman). When he finds a wounded German Shepherd in the woods, he tries to nurse the dog back to health and keep him a secret at the same time. (Back home, Chris reads a dog book which appears to feature a photograph of Charles Eisenmann's London.) An unpleasant encounter with his cousin, a bad storm, and the dog's worsening condition all lead Chris to eventually confess about the dog and seek Cal's help to bring him home and take care of him. Cal does not want the dog on their sheep farm, but he sees how much Smoke means to Chris and agrees he can keep Smoke as long as no one claims him after they run an ad in the paper. Someone does come for the dog and Chris finds that his and Smoke's problems have only just begun.

The trainer for *Smoke* is unknown, though the movie has a considerable amount of coyote footage, and the coyotes—if not the dog as well—were almost certainly trained by Lloyd Beebe of Walt Disney's Wild Animal Ranch in Sequim, Washington. The name was changed to the Olympic Game Farm in 1972. In the two long fight scenes between the German Shepherd and the coyotes, the dog wore a wire muzzle to protect the smaller animals, though the coyotes did not have on the same.

Azit, the Paratrooper Dog (1972)

Also known as *Azit Hakalba Hatzanhanit*
GSD: *Azit*
Trainer: Moshe Engelberg
Director: Boaz Davidson
Costars: Yossi Pollack, Mona Zelberstein
Country: Israel
Status: Limited availability

Azit, the Paratrooper Dog, or *Azit: Canine Paratrooper*, was based on a children's book by Mordechai "Motta" Gur, former Israeli chief of staff. *Azit* was referenced in *Traditions in*

World Cinema as an example of films stereotyping both Israelis and Arabs—the former in a positive light and the latter in a negative one. Although Azit was a fictional character, there have been parachuting war dogs for many years. During World War II, many armies used parachuting dogs with special harnesses and chutes. There are still dogs being used in airborne units today.

Azit is a normal dog belonging to Tami Haruvi (Mona Zelberstein) until a chance encounter changes their lives: the local butcher and his wife, who are both afraid of Azit, run into trouble with a thief, and Azit comes to the rescue, tracking the man through neighborhoods and over high walls to retrieve the stolen purse. Tami's friend, Lieutenant Ori (Yossi Pollack), knowing what happened, takes Azit into military training, and she joins a parachuting troop. After training, Azit makes a parachute jump into desert territory controlled by an Arab gang. Later, she is launched into increasingly dangerous missions.

Azit is played by an athletic male GSD, trained by Moshe Engelberg, one of the most renowned trainers in Israel and owner of Uncle Moshe's Farm, a large boarding and training facility. Like *Legend of the Northwest*, *Azit* begins with a song over the opening credits:

> *Azit, the best dog in the world,*
> *She's a dog who is great,*
> *She's a dog who is royal,*
> *Nowhere will you find a dog who's so loyal,*

Into danger she dives,
She saves many lives.

The Call of the Wild (1972)

GSD: *Buck*
Trainer: Unknown
Director: Ken Annakin
Costars: Charlton Heston, Raimund Harmstorf
Countries: France, Germany, Italy, Norway, Spain, UK, USA
Status: Available on DVD

This is probably the best known of the many film adaptations of Jack London's classic novel, *The Call of the Wild.* Filmed in Norway, Finland, and Spain, the crew had to endure climates and terrain as challenging as any of those faced by the characters in the book. Though most of the film was shot in Norway, the sled dogs, acting dogs, and trainers all had to be brought from outside the country. Many of the dogs were extremely aggressive toward each other—like the packs in London's novel—and a lot of time was spent breaking up unscripted fights.

The movie opens with a group of Siberian Huskies led by a German Shepherd, Buck, as they pursue and drag down a caribou from a herd of hundreds. After this, the first half hour is surprisingly true to the novel, following Buck's passage from his comfortable California home to the Arctic and his rise to the leader of the sled team. He must kill his rival, Spitz, played by a solid black GSD (though he resembles a Samoyed in the book), to achieve this. Buck and his teammates pass from master to master, worn and beaten down as they travel back and forth along the trail that leads from Skagway to Dawson City during the 1897–1898 Yukon gold rush. Buck eventually grows healthy and strong again under the care of John Thornton (Charlton Heston), and the dog turns his back on civilization to answer the call of the wild.

As a boy, Charlton Heston had a Shepherd, Lobo, with whom he used to pretend he was enacting *The Call of the Wild*: the dog was large enough to pull him around on a small sled. After Heston starred as John Thornton, he thought of the film as being his worst ever—though he enjoyed working with the main German Shepherd in the film and said he was the best actor in it. His daughter, Holly, also met Buck. Holly was on set one day during the filming of a scene in which both Thornton and Buck fall through ice. When the scene cut, Holly raced in, desperate to make sure the dog, not her father, was okay.

Lone Wolf (1972)

Also known as *Vuk samotnjak*

GSD: *Hund*

Trainer: Unknown

Director: Obrad Gluscevic

Costars: Slavko Stimac, Boro Ivanisevic

Country: Yugoslavia

Status: Limited availability

Lone Wolf, or *The Lone Wolf*, was a Yugoslavian children's film shown on television in the United States as part of the *CBS Children's Film Festival*. The show brought dozens of foreign films to U.S. children in the 1960s and 1970s. A large number of the films were about dogs, including *Doggie and Three* (1955, Czechoslovakia), *Flash the Sheepdog* (1966, UK), *Clown* (1969, Spain), *Friends for Life* (1971, Soviet Union), *Where's Johnny?* (1974, UK), and many others.

A young boy named Ranko (Slavko Stimac) befriends a German Shepherd after he finds the dog caught in a trap. The dog's collar identifies him as a military "Hund." Ranko has been told that the German military dogs are killers and "worse than wolves," but he finds Hund to be not at all like the stories he has heard. He decides to take the dog home with him but first returns home for his sled, since Hund is too injured to walk far. He tells his father and grandmother about meeting the dog, and after first thinking he is lying, his father believes him and sets out with other men in the town to shoot Hund. After Hund saves Ranko from wolves, he is still an outcast, but Ranko saves Hund in return and is able to show the townspeople what a gentle dog he is.

Eurasian wolves are seen in the film. The wolves slink around the sheep pens looking for a way in. When one is shot and the body is carried around by a hunter, it is a stiff, taxidermic animal. Though the dog fights them away from Ranko, this is not shown on camera.

Lone Wolf originally aired on CBS on September 22, 1973. An edited and poorly dubbed version was released on VHS through Children's Treasures—which released such films as *Alice Through the Looking Glass* (1966)—along with Janus Films, known for distributing art-house and classic films from around the world.

White Fang (1973)

Also known as *Zanna Bianca*
GSD: *White Fang*
Trainer: Sebastiano Arsifa (unconfirmed)
Director: Lucio Fulci
Costars: Franco Nero, John Steiner
Countries: France, Italy, Spain
Status: Limited availability

This spaghetti western, set up as the sequel to *The Call of the Wild* (see page 118), was directed by infamous Italian horror master Lucio Fulci long before his films were being banned all over Europe. One of his most famous cult films, *The Beyond* (1981), also featured a German Shepherd, as a bloodthirsty guide dog named Dickie. Fulci's influence is noticeable here: The title dog is shown covered from head to tail in neon blood after a fight with a bear. He later kills a man by savaging his throat—something Hollywood canines only do if the dog himself is the bad guy.

White Fang is found in the forest by a native hunter, Charlie (Daniel Martín), and his son Mitsah (Missaele). When the boy becomes ill, Charlie takes him downriver to town in search of a doctor. White Fang follows them and lands in a fight as soon as he reaches town. "Beauty" Smith (John Steiner), the evil overlord of the town, tries to buy the dog from Charlie, then has Charlie killed when he won't sell. Sister Evangelina (Virna Lisi) and good guys Jason Scott (Franco Nero) and his sidekick (Raimund Harmstorf, returning from *The Call of the Wild*) step in to save White Fang from a fight against a bear, then take back the town from Smith's clutches with White Fang's help.

Most or all of the Italian *White Fang* films employed trainer Sebastiano Arsifa, though it is unconfirmed that Arsifa did the first one. Dogs who played the role included Saccha and Habbash. As with other Euro westerns of the time, the treatment of the animals is often brutal. Even today, there is no agency in Europe that monitors how animals are treated on film sets.

Fulci went on to direct one more *White Fang* film in 1974, *Challenge to White Fang*, again showing his propensity toward gore effects. Other directors handled the string of five more European-produced *White Fang* films made in the 1970s. All together, there have been twelve live-action feature films based on *White Fang* and a live-action TV show.

The Billion Dollar Hobo (1974)

GSD: Bo as himself
Trainer: Charles P. Eisenmann
Director: Stuart E. McGowan
Costars: Tim Conway, Will Geer
Country: USA
Status: Available on DVD

After Charles Eisenmann's dogs stopped appearing in the original *Littlest Hobo* television show, they could still be seen in thousands of public appearances, several films such as *Just Between Us* (1961) and *Silent Friends* (1969), and dozens of television shows, including *The Waltons*, *The Merv Griffin Show*, *The Tonight Show*, and *The Today Show*. In 1974, one of Eisenmann's extraordinary German Shepherds landed another starring film role.

The dog in *The Billion Dollar Hobo* is played by Bo. For the first two years of his life, Bo did not bark. He remained reticent until Eisenmann found himself with a dilemma: Toro had to have a surgical procedure done around a shoot, and Bo was the best dog to take his place, but he needed to bark. Normal methods of teaching Bo to bark on cue failed. It took a raccoon tail the dog found fascinating to get him to use his voice for the first time. Within a day, Eisenmann was able to remove the tail from the scenario altogether and cue Bo verbally to bark. He is credited as "Bo, the World's Smartest Dog." This claim had been made of other performing dogs in the past—however, with Eisenmann's dogs, it was probably true.

The Billion Dollar Hobo stars Tim Conway as Vernon Praiseworthy, a bumbling short-order cook who stands to inherit an enormous fortune from a man he didn't even know he was related to: Choo-Choo Trayne (Will Geer), who tells Vernon he first must demonstrate his abilities by riding the rails as a hobo. But Choo-Choo is too smart to let Vernon try it on his own—he sends his dog, Bo, along with Vernon to take care of any necessary thinking. Vernon hops on the wrong train, gets a ride from a gang of dognappers, then finds himself involved in the theft of a prized Shar-Pei who just arrived in the country from China. Bo does his best to keep things under control, rescuing both Vernon and the dognapped dog, but it's not easy when his traveling companion makes more mistakes than Inspector Clouseau.

Lions for Breakfast (1974)

GSD: Atlas as *Moby*
Trainer: Marvin Kelso
Director: William Davidson
Costars: Danny Forbes, Jan Rubes
Country: Canada
Status: Limited availability

Atlas of Marvinsway plays Moby in this independent Canadian film. Atlas was selected by a Toronto talent scout to audition for *Lions for Breakfast* while he was at a ceremony to receive an award in obedience. He was an eager-to-please and extremely talented German Shepherd whom trainer Marvin Kelso knew could have taken on a much more complex role. Among Atlas's many skills were leaping through paper or fire hoops, walking a balance beam, and untying knots.

Zanny (Danny Forbes) watches a man's dog at a market and takes the dog home when the man does not return. He finds his older brother, Trick (Jim Henshaw), leaving in search of "The Blue," a haven he longs for since their parents have been gone. Zanny takes off with the dog (Atlas) to follow his brother. They spot the dog's owner getting into a bus and driving away. Later, the dog finds the man, Count Ivan Stroganoff (Jan Rubes). Zanny joins him and Stroganoff tells him the dog's name is Moby, after Mobile, Alabama. They find Trick and all four start out for The Blue together, guided by the address on a deed that Ivan won in a game of cards. Along the way, they encounter country auctions, African safari parks, and a thief who steals their bus.

In the bus-stealing scene, Moby sleeps through the theft before waking and alerting the humans while the bus is being driven off. Kelso argued against this, saying no German Shepherd would let such a thing happen right under his nose. But the original script won out, and the resulting scene is quite unbelievable. Atlas holds a special place in the hearts of Marvin Kelso and his wife, Barbara: he was in the first German Shepherd litter they bred and was raised by them from birth, being fondly remembered as a once-in-a-lifetime dog. Atlas died at eleven of spondylosis after appearing on TV, as well as having a single scene in one other film: *Off Your Rocker* (1982).

Atlas poses for the camera. (Author's collection)

The Great Adventure (1975)

Also known as *Il Richiamo del lupo*

GSD: *Buck*

Trainer: Unknown

Director: Gianfranco Baldanello

Costars: Jack Palance, Joan Collins

Countries: Italy, Spain

Status: Available on DVD

Once again, a film that bears little resemblance to one of Jack London's novels is supposedly both the sequel to *The Call of the Wild* and based on *White Fang*. The same dog sled team that is seen at the beginning of *The Great Adventure* appeared in 1972's *The Call of the Wild* (see page 118). Several other things, such as the scenes in which the dogs chase caribou, appear to be nearly identical to footage from *The Call of the Wild*.

A boy named Jim (Fernando E. Romero, credited as Fred Romer) finds a German Shepherd. His father believes the dog is a famed sled dog who had returned to the wild after his master was killed: Buck. Two gold prospectors lose their sled team after an accident and make their way to Jim's cabin. Jim and his sister are alone with Buck—their father has gone to Dawson to get supplies. The men, brothers John (Manuel de Blas) and Hank (Remo De Angelis), start toward Dawson with Buck and the children after they find their father's dead body. They are separated and Hank is killed by the men of evil William Bates (Jack Palance) when they reach

Dawson. After Buck and the kids arrive, they all work to overthrow Bates.

The Great Adventure was another spaghetti western with a known American actor, just like *The Call of the Wild* with Charlton Heston, as well as the most famous of all spaghetti westerns: *The Good, the Bad and the Ugly* (1966) with Clint Eastwood. The original Italian title translates literally to *The Callback of the Wolf*, and the English European title is *The Cry of the Wolf*. Only for the American release was the whole wolf concept dropped and the title changed to *The Great Adventure*.

Won Ton Ton, the Dog Who Saved Hollywood (1976)

GSD: Gus as *Won Ton Ton*
Trainer: Karl Lewis Miller
Director: Michael Winner
Costars: Madeline Kahn, Bruce Dern
Country: USA
Status: Available on DVD

Karl Lewis Miller had already been training dogs and other animals for film and TV for many years when he got the job on *Won Ton Ton, the Dog Who Saved Hollywood*. Miller worked with well known trainers such as Frank Inn, of Benji fame, and Lou Schumacher, who was working with him while he was head trainer on *Won Ton Ton* and *The Pack* (see page 132). Miller trained German Shepherd Dogs for TV shows like *Longstreet* (1971–1972) and its TV-movie tie-in, and *Run, Joe, Run* (1974), forming his own company, Animal Action, in 1978. The starring dog in *Won Ton Ton*, Augustus von Schumacher (call name Gus), was the double in *Run, Joe, Run* before he got the Won Ton Ton part out of over one hundred German Shepherds to audition.

Gus, a 96-pound, black and tan GSD from German lines, was born on November 29, 1972. He was trained to jump through breakaway brick walls and run with fake lit dynamite in his mouth for the film and even won a PATSY Award for it. To get an intent look on his face during the chaos of filming on a set, Miller drew his eye with a live hamster in a cage which fascinated the dog. When filming wrapped, Gus attended a lavish Hollywood party in his honor and later appeared in the Tournament of Roses Parade, where he wore a Tiffany diamond collar worth $250,000.

The film is something of a cross between a remake of *Kelly and Me* (see page 91) and *Hollywood Cavalcade*. Both spoof the career of the original Rin-Tin-Tin, as well as 1920s Hollywood in general. It follows a German Shepherd (Gus) who escapes gassing at a city pound and falls in love with an aspiring actress, Estie Del Ruth (Madeline Kahn). When the dog—whom tour-guide-turned-screenwriter-and-director Grayson Potchuck (Bruce Dern) names Won Ton Ton—finds himself as the next big Hollywood star, Estie becomes an unwilling dog trainer. Estie at last gets her own wish of starring opposite superstar Rudy Montague (Ron Leibman), only to wish she had let the dog keep the limelight as her own film bombs.

Strongheart fans will enjoy Won Ton Ton's screening party in the movie: an original clip of the Strongheart film *The Return of Boston Blackie* (see page 18) is shown.

The Hills Have Eyes (1977)

GSD: Striker as *Beast*
Trainer: Moe Disesso
Director: Wes Craven
Costars: Robert Houston, Susan Lanier
Country: USA
Status: Available on DVD

The hero of *The Hills Have Eyes* is the blanket back German Shepherd named Striker. Striker belonged to Moe Disesso, who worked with many GSDs in film and TV. He was perhaps best known for training the rats of *Willard* (1971) and *Ben* (1972), winning a PATSY Award for each.

A family on vacation in their RV finds itself stranded in the middle of a former nuclear-testing zone many miles from civilization. Unknown to them, there are savage people in the hills who start picking them off one by one in gruesome attacks. The first line of defense for the family members is not their guns, it's their super-smart German Shepherd Dog, Beast (Striker). A second German Shepherd Beauty (Flora), is one of the first victims of the attacks, and Beast makes it his mission to avenge her death. While the villains get the upper hand again and again, Beast takes them out one after the other, even bringing a handheld transceiver of theirs back to his family so they can eavesdrop on the killers' plans.

There is an unusual message at the end of *Hills* that does not come from the AHA or any other organization: "No animals were destroyed or inhumanly treated in the making of this film." However, the body of a dead dog is seen on film, which the producers acquired from the county in California where they were filming.

Multiple dogs played the roles of the two German Shepherds—one of which, Bracket, doubled as the bionic dog in the television series *The Bionic Woman* (1976–1978). Eight years later, a sequel, *The Hills Have Eyes Part II* (1985) was released. In it, Beast is back, but he is played by a GSD who does not look like the original. The most memorable scene in the film is the dog having his own flashback to footage from the original movie as Beast remembers attacking the bad guys.

The Pack (1977)

GSD: Heinrich as *Rye*

Trainer: Karl Lewis Miller

Director: Robert Clouse

Costars: Joe Don Baker, Hope Alexander-Willis

Country: USA

Status: Limited availability

The Pack, based on David Fisher's novel, was retitled *The Long, Dark Night* before being changed back right before release. Along with other killer animal movies like *Dogs* (1976) and *Day of the Animals* (1977), it launched a new era of dog films: horror. There had always been killer dogs off and on in movies, but by the late 1970s, Hollywood could not seem to get enough of these bad dogs. The original script for *The Pack* got a little carried away with things like canine makeup: for example, it said that the pack's leader was missing an ear and had a huge scar across his head. Although the dog did end up with some makeup effects in the film, he kept both ears.

The story centers around a few local residents of a small island and a vacationing family. Dogs who have been abandoned by tourists over the summer are now starving and crazed as they form into a pack and begin hunting down the humans. The pack is led by a large, brown mixed breed. Among others in the pack, there are mixes, a Collie, a Dalmatian, an Irish Setter, a Doberman Pinscher, and several German Shepherds, including one white and one long-haired. There are also two dogs in the film who are playing for the good guys. Both are black and tan German Shepherds: Rye (Heinrich), who belongs to human hero Jerry (Joe Don Baker), and Zsa Zsa, a guide dog who becomes one of the first casualties of the pack.

Karl Lewis Miller demonstrated here the genius he had for bringing out frightening behaviors and expressions in dogs. In several scenes, the leader of the dog pack has a device in his mouth which was designed to press the lips upward and create an extreme snarl. Miller used this again to great effect in *Dracula's Dog*. Miller worked with toy-motivated dogs to get them to throw themselves at car windshields and dig while also responding to commands to show their teeth. The brown leader in *The Pack* performs the exact same action that Daddy, another of Miller's dogs, was to later exhibit in *Cujo* (1983), the best known canine horror film ever. When trying to break into the car, all Daddy was really working for was a squeaky mouse.

Devil Dog: The Hound of Hell (1978)

GSD: *Lucky*

Trainer: Moe Disesso

Director: Curtis Harrington

Costars: Richard Crenna, Yvette Mimieux

Country: USA

Status: Available on DVD

Devil Dog: The Hound of Hell is a made-for-TV movie that originally aired on CBS on Halloween night 1978. The low budget of this film is particularly noticeable in the special effects shots, which look like they were thrown together one evening in someone's basement. Curtis Harrington wanted to use a Rottweiler for *Devil Dog*, but animal trainer Moe Disesso talked him out of it on the grounds that the only breed well suited for the complexity of the role was a German Shepherd. The dog who plays Lucky was also one of the dogs who appeared as Maximillion in the third and final season of *The Bionic Woman.*

When a devil-worshiping cult buys a $5,000 female German Shepherd to breed with a demon, one of the resulting ten puppies finds a home with the Berry family. Only the maid, Maria (Tina Menard), recognizes something evil in Lucky. Using the force of his mind, Lucky wreaks havoc, first killing Maria. He grows up to possess the children, Charlie (Ike Eisenmann) and Bonnie (Kim Richards); almost forces their father, Michael (Richard Crenna), to put his hand into a running lawnmower blade; and then kills both their neighbor and his Great Dane. By the time Michael confronts his wife (Yvette Mimieux) about the dog, it's too late—Lucky has her under his control. Michael must find out the truth and destroy the demon himself.

Devil Dog is possibly the only canine horror film in which the dog not only never bites anyone, but never even tries to attack. Lucky uses his gaze (Disesso held a ball off-camera to achieve this) and telepathy to get what he wants. Even when he is shown as a horned canine from hell, he only snaps his jaws and wags his tail. Director Curtis Harrington said that when he read the script, he found it "ridiculous." However, he was in need of the job, and he did *Devil Dog* reluctantly.

Good Dog/Bad Dog: The 1980s

There was a great deal of new ground covered with German Shepherd Dog films of the 1980s, including some stories not seen before. In 1982, Sam Fuller brought to life the horrors of "white dogs" with a powerful anti-racist film, which was not commercially released in the United States until nine years later. Disney once more worked with German Shepherds to tell one of the most extraordinary true stories of a GSD in history. In England, a beautiful, long-coated Shepherd formed the center of an unusual love triangle, and in the U.S. a dog formed a love/hate relationship with a cop in a PG-13 buddy movie. The GSDs of 1980s films flip back and forth from loyal friends to villains, sometimes within the same movie.

The Courage of Kavik, the Wolf Dog (1980)

Also known as *Kavik: The Wolf Dog*

GSD: Heinrich as *Kavik*

Trainer: Karl Lewis Miller

Director: Peter Carter

Costars: Andrew Ian McMillan, Ronny Cox

Country: Canada

Status: Available on DVD

Based on the juvenile novel *Kavik, the Wolf Dog,* by Walt Morey, *The Courage of Kavik, the Wolf Dog* was a made-for-TV movie that first aired on Sunday night, January 20, 1980. It was rebroadcast on August 31 of the same year. When the film was released on VHS, and later, DVD, it came out under the title, *Kavik: The Wolf Dog.*

Kavik—meaning "wolverine"—is a journey story, common in dog films: *Lassie Come Home* (1943), *Poco . . . Little Dog Lost* (1977), *Hambone & Hillie* (1983), and *Homeward Bound: The Incredible Journey* (1993) are just a few. It is Kavik who possibly faces the toughest challenges of all. His is the only one of these stories in which the dog must cross arctic landscapes to reach home. *Kavik* is also the only one of these movies to star a GSD, though there is a white German Shepherd in a supporting role in *Hambone & Hillie.*

Wealthy George Hunter (John Ireland) buys a prized sled dog, Kavik (Heinrich), to bring home to Seattle as a sort of Alaskan souvenir. The bush plane transporting the dog crashes. Kavik is rescued and nursed back to health by a boy named Andy (Andrew Ian McMillan) who lives in a small town in Alaska. Hunter eventually finds out and comes to claim his dog, but in Seattle, Kavik spooks at a party Hunter throws in his honor, crashes through a window, and takes off north. The dog finds dog catchers, hunters, wolves, and the elements against him as he crosses 2,000 miles in search of the boy he loves.

Heinrich, who played Kavik, belonged to producer William D'Angelo and was trained by Karl Lewis Miller. Heinrich also starred as Rye in *The Pack* (see page 132) and was the lead dog for the short-lived TV series *Run, Joe, Run*. A real wolf is used in a scene where Kavik, having been traumatized by the plane crash, fights to victory and reclaims his courage. The wolf wore a wire muzzle but still overpowered the dog. Additional wires were fastened around the wolf's limbs and pulled in front to trip it and keep the two animals from becoming too closely tangled together.

Klondike Fever (1980)

GSD: *Buck*
Trainer: Karl Lewis Miller
Director: Peter Carter
Costars: Jeff East, Rod Steiger
Country: Canada
Status: Available on DVD

Klondike Fever revisited a story from the 1943 film *Jack London*, relating a fictional account of Jack London's trip to the Yukon in the gold rush of 1897–1898. The title is the same as Pierre Berton's history of the rush published in 1958, though the two are otherwise unrelated. Another of Karl Lewis Miller's German Shepherds starred in *Klondike Fever*. Strangely, the dog gets very little screen time, though the whole plot revolves around him.

Jack London (Jeff East) arrives in Skagway in 1897 and encounters a man beating a dog while a crowd looks on. London intervenes and walks off with the German Shepherd, Buck, then tries to buy him from the owner, Soapy Smith (Rod Steiger). Smith asks $300 for the dog. London wins the money at cards, but Smith refuses to take it, saying he wants the dog back. London knows he has made a dangerous enemy yet will not give up Buck. He leaves town with Buck and his partner, Merritt Sloper (Robin Gammell). They stake a claim at Stewart Creek and both get cabin fever before Soapy's men catch up with them and Sloper is shot. London rushes him to Dawson City only to find Soapy already there. They settle the ownership of Buck by running a dogsled race with Buck leading London's team.

Klondike Fever spins what could have been a fast-paced, exciting man-and-his-dog story into a monotonous slog through the Yukon. The film needs an hour cut from the almost two-hour running time and a new score to improve it. The short-haired, black and tan Shepherd has a few moments of greatness but cannot compensate for Jeff East's painful overacting or terrible dialogue.

White Dog (1982)

GSD: Hans as the white dog
Trainer: Karl Lewis Miller
Director: Samuel Fuller
Costars: Kristy McNichol, Paul Winfield
Country: USA
Status: Available on DVD

White Dog is based on a story and subsequent novel, inspired by true events, by Romain Gary. Although it is an anti-racist film, *White Dog* was the target of controversy claiming it was the very opposite. Even with financial backing by Paramount, it was widely released only in Europe until 1991, when it at last reached American theaters. In 1984, NBC planned to show *White Dog* on its network but abruptly dropped the film, saying it would be "inappropriate for us to broadcast it." It was not until 2008 that The Criterion Collection released *White Dog* in its full unedited and restored form for the first time on DVD.

Julie Sawyer (Kristy McNichol) hits a white German Shepherd with her car one night and takes him home. She posts Found signs around town before he saves her from a rapist (played by trainer Karl Lewis Miller). She changes her mind about keeping him, only to discover later that he has a killer side: he's a "white dog," trained to viciously attack black people. Sawyer wants to retrain the dog. She finds someone willing to try in the form of Keys (Paul Winfield), who has tried twice before to break white dogs. The stakes get higher after the dog escapes and kills a man, yet Keys refuses to give up, desperate to prove that racism can be defeated.

Karl Lewis Miller trained a five-dog team to play the part of the unnamed dog in the film. The two leading canines were Hans (sometimes called Heinz) and Folsom. They were the "actor" dogs who worked with the human actors and did close-ups. The other three—Son, Buster, and Duke—were protection dogs used interchangeably for attacks and stunts. Though Sam Fuller wanted to use dark German Shepherds, since the title does not refer to the dog's color, Paramount had already asked Miller to begin training white Shepherds. Miller perfected many techniques working on *White Dog*, including high attack jumps off platforms.

Extensive use of the device that is placed inside the dog's mouth to press the lips up can also be found here.

Love Leads the Way (1984)

GSD: Pilot as *Buddy*
Trainer: Ron Bledsoe
Director: Delbert Mann
Costars: Timothy Bottoms, Eva Marie Saint
Country: USA
Status: Limited availability

Love Leads the Way was one of the first Disney Channel movies. It is based on the book *First Lady of the Seeing Eye*, by Morris Frank and Blake Clark: an autobiography of Morris Frank and the first U.S. guide dog, Buddy—a sable, female German Shepherd Dog—and how the two helped to found The Seeing Eye, Inc. Producer Jimmy Hawkins first pitched the idea of adapting the book as a TV movie to CBS, NBC, ABC, and others. They all refused to back what they saw as a "malady" film.

It's 1924 when Morris Frank (Timothy Bottoms) is blinded in a boxing accident. Four years later, he discovers an article in the *Saturday Evening Post* by an American, Dorothy Eustis (Eva Marie Saint), who is living in Switzerland and has witnessed the amazing training process for some German

Shepherd Dogs learning to guide soldiers blinded in World War I. Frank writes her a letter explaining that he would like to learn to work with one of these remarkable dogs and teach others back in America how to do so as well. Mrs. Eustis invites Frank to Switzerland where, along with trainer Jack Humphrey (Gerald Hiken) and Buddy (Pilot), she changes his life. When Frank returns to his home of Nashville, Tennessee, he finds that the challenges are only just beginning for him and his new guide. His dog is not allowed on buses, trains, planes, or in shops or restaurants. But Morris is ready to fight to change all that.

Pilot, trained by Ron Bledsoe of Nashville, Tennessee, receives the first billing in the closing credits. The adviser for the film from The Seeing Eye was Ned Myrose. The film focuses too much on Frank's early life, including a great deal of time before he even meets Buddy. It picks up considerably after that and concludes with a suspenseful and emotional ending. Buddy died on Christmas Day 1938, leaving behind a legacy immortalized by the work that The Seeing Eye began in 1929 and continues today.

Red Riding Hood (1987)

GSD: *Dagger*

Trainer: Ze'ev Bengali

Director: Adam Brooks

Costars: Amelia Shankley, Isabella Rossellini

Countries: Israel, USA

Status: Available on DVD

The trainer of the long-haired German Shepherd Dog featured in *Red Riding Hood* is listed in the credits under "Wolf Wrangler." The "wolf" in this version of the Brothers Grimm's *Little Red Riding Hood* is played alternately by a man and dog. A real wolf, or even a hybrid, is never seen. This was not the first time the story had been told on screen with a German Shepherd. *Little Red Riding Hood* of 1922 featured Peter the Great as the wolf.

There is much back story here before Linet (Amelia Shankley) actually takes a basket of food to her grand-mother's house and encounters a wolf in the woman's place. This back story involves the main characters: Linet's mother (Isabella Rossellini) and grandmother (Helen Glazary); the evil overlord Godfrey (Craig T. Nelson); and Dagger (Rocco Sisto), his henchman, who he can turn from wolf to human with his "black magic." They all burst into song at strange moments in order to convey whatever they might be think-ing. It is too bad none of them can carry a tune. Fortunately, Dagger's stints as the handsome, long-haired, black sable GSD add a great deal to the film. The dog gets several solo shots as he stalks his victim, then runs from angry townspeople in turns. In the end, the evil Godfrey is driven out of town. As he staggers away, his shoulders hunch, his body shakes, and he turns into a wolf (the same dog who played the doomed Dagger), which races out of town.

Red Riding Hood was filmed in Israel and released in the U.S. by Cannon. In 1989, it came out on VHS along with other films like *Sleeping Beauty* (1987) and *Snow White* (1987) under the label *Cannon Movie Tales*. In 1994, it aired on the Disney Channel and was eventually picked up by MGM for DVD release. The *Cannon Movie Tales* series of fairy-tale films is still fondly remembered today by many fans.

We Think the World of You (1988)

GSD: Betsy as *Evie*
Trainer: Unknown (see description)
Director: Colin Gregg
Costars: Alan Bates, Gary Oldman
Country: UK
Status: Limited availability

One of the most beautiful creatures ever to grace the screen appears in this British film based on J.R. Ackerley's 1960 novel of the same name. Betsy, who played the heroine of the story, was an eighteen-month-old, privately owned, long-coated German Shepherd. She was trained for the part by a company called Animals Galore, now run by Cindy Newman in Horley, Surrey, England, though no individual trainer is credited. *We Think the World of You* is a fictionalized but somewhat autobiographical account of Ackerley's own experiences with his German Shepherd. Ackerley wrote about his dog in the classic canine memoir, *My Dog Tulip*, which has been adapted into an animated film.

Frank (Alan Bates) has trouble finding time to spend with his lover, Johnny (Gary Oldman), due to their class and address differences and Johnny's wife, Megan (Frances Barber). Things get worse when Johnny is sent to prison for breaking and entering. Johnny's German Shepherd puppy goes to live with his mother and stepfather while he is away. When Frank meets Evie (Betsy), he realizes that she has been living in awful conditions with Johnny's parents, closed in a tiny cement yard for months and hardly ever getting out. He offers to take her out and later to take her home, then finds himself fighting for time with her. Evie is untrained and un-socialized after growing up mostly in the tiny yard. Soon, Frank is willing to put everything else aside—his career, his social life, and even Johnny—to take care of a dog who does not even belong to him.

Despite its many charms, the film fails to capture the emotional intensity of the first-person novel, but it is other-wise a faithful adaptation. It received overall good reviews with its December 1988 release in New York. *The Boston Globe* said it hosted "a screenful of delicious performances." *The New York Times* summed it up with this: "The craziest plot of the season belongs, without question, to this story of two Englishmen who are in love with each other and, more significantly, with the same dog." The film has yet to be released on DVD.

Betsy and Alan Bates on the set of *We Think the World of You.* (Author's collection)

K-9 (1989)

GSD: Rando as *Jerry Lee*
Trainer: Karl Lewis Miller
Director: Rod Daniel
Costars: James Belushi, Mel Harris
Country: USA
Status: Available on DVD

After looking at dozens of dogs for the part of Jerry Lee, Karl Lewis Miller asked *K-9* technical adviser Mark Mooring, who was part of the Los Angeles K-9 unit, to bring back dogs from Germany with star potential. A dog named Rando was selected to play Jerry Lee while the others played his stunt doubles. They did not understand English and Miller had only twelve weeks to train the eighteen-month-old dogs. Luckily, a writers' strike put off production for another fourteen weeks, giving him additional training time. Rando has often been wrongly credited as Koton. Koton was a working police dog who appeared in the unsold 1991 TV spinoff of *K-9* by the same title.

Unorthodox detective Thomas Dooley (James Belushi) finds himself in a bind when he needs to search a warehouse for drugs. He asks for help from the K-9 unit and ends up with a dog on loan who has some personality issues. Dooley and Jerry Lee (Rando) hit the streets together to track down a drug lord, but neither of the two partners are in the spirit of the mission as, one after the other, they test each other's patience and intelligence. For example, Dooley takes the dog, who lives on a diet of chili, through a car wash in his convertible. In retaliation, Jerry Lee rips the radio system out of his car. The enduring tagline is brought home many times in this buddy film: *One's just a little smarter than the other.*

With the exception of horror films, *K-9* is one of the few modern examples of dog movies marketed toward adults. Director Rod Daniel was unusually accommodating to Miller, starting each day's work by asking where he needed to be for the shots and how to best set up, whereas trainers are often the last to know how something will be shot. A fake dog was used in a few scenes, such as a dangerous car chase, but Rando and his doubles did most of their own stunt work, including riding through a specially prepared car wash after both Miller and an AHA representative rode through first.

K-9000 (1989)

GSD: *Niner*
Trainer: Roger Schumacher
Director: Kim Manners
Costars: Chris Mulkey, Catherine Oxenberg
Country: USA
Status: Available on DVD (PAL format only)

This made-for-TV movie was produced in 1989 but not released until 1991. Roger Schumacher, the son of Lou

Schumacher, was the head trainer for *K-9000*. The German Shepherd came from Gary Gero's Birds & Animals Unlimited when it was still a relatively small company, having worked on *Never Cry Wolf* (1983) and *Ladyhawke* (1985), but long before it became better known for such epic animal film projects as *101 Dalmatians* (1996), *Eight Below* (2006), and the *Harry Potter* series.

Eddie Monroe (Chris Mulkey) is a cop with an anger management problem and a distaste for anything mechanical. After a high-speed car chase gone wrong, he is demoted to giving out traffic tickets. Monroe's life takes a turn when he becomes involved in the robbery of top-secret, experimental technology in the form of K-9000, a cybernetic German Shepherd. Monroe and one of the veterinarians who had been developing K-9000, Aja Turner (Catherine Oxenberg), recover the technology at the moment the dog is leaving the "cocoon," and Monroe is inadvertently implanted with a microchip allowing "Niner" to speak to him. Niner (voiced by Jerry Houser) helps Monroe crack the case, saving the man's life a couple of times along the way.

Although the GSD does not arrive until forty minutes into the ninety-minute film, and in the meantime, you have to listen to bad dialogue from mediocre actors while looking at Chris Mulkey's mullet, this cyber-dog is worth the wait. Niner is played by an unusual-looking, as well as talented, dog with striking facial markings. His performance is one seldom matched in a made-for-TV film; he holds a mark and eye line for extended periods of time, then moves from point A to point B while his trainer may be extremely far away or not visible to the dog.

Diverse Decade: The 1990s

Independent films and made-for-TV movies were booming in the 1990s. Half of all the films profiled in this decade are made-for-TV and are diverse as films themselves. There are police dogs, war dogs, sled dogs, children's protectors, killers, and even a boy who becomes a dog in the German Shepherd films of the 1990s. This decade brought us some of the best known and highest grossing animal films ever, including *Beethoven* (1992), *Babe* (1995), and *101 Dalmatians*, which grossed over $136 million.

The Paris Conspiracy (1991)

Also known as *Rin Tin Tin and the Paris Conspiracy*

GSD: Ike as *Rudy / Rinty*

Trainer: Bryan Renfro

Directors: Dennis Berry, Alain Nahum

Costars: Jesse Collins, Denise Virieux

Country: Canada

Status: Rare

The Canadian television series *Katts and Dog* ran for five seasons, from 1988 to 1993. One made-for-TV movie, *The Paris Conspiracy*, also came from the show about Officer Hank Katts and his K-9 partner, Rudy. In the United States, the series was released as *Rin Tin Tin: K-9 Cop*. Also in the U.S., the movie aired as *Rin Tin Tin and the Paris Conspiracy*. Since the dog's name was Rudy originally, his name was redubbed throughout the show and film as *Rinty* before being released in the U.S. The show proved to be a big hit in Europe, especially in Germany and France, where it is available in DVD boxed sets under the title *Rintintin Junior*.

First broadcast on The Family Channel (now ABC Family) on November 23, 1991, the film has Officer Katts (Jesse Collins) and Rudy (Ike) at a convention in France when the two are called into service. What starts as a murder and diamond theft soon becomes a nuclear weapons conspiracy as the pair race against the clock to save Katts's nephew, Stevie (Andrew Bednarski), and bring down terrorists. The work from the dog is exceptional. There are many long angles and long scenes without cuts where Rudy must stay with the actors or work on his own.

The dogs playing Rudy/Rinty were no relation to the Rin-Tin-Tin line. The dog that starred in the TV show's first season was Rocky. He was replaced in the second season, and for the film, by Ike, a dog from Germany. Ike's doubles included Luke, for running and jumping, and a dog named X, who did attack scenes. Others were Cora and Jesse, who shared a name with the starring human. Jesse Collins became close friends with both the dogs and trainers during production.

Bryan Renfro, son of one of the best known film trainers in Hollywood during the 1930s, worked alongside Roger Schumacher for the show, but is credited as head trainer for the film. Both were working for Birds & Animals Unlimited at the time. Some of the film was actually shot in France, where the trainers paid a visit to the original Rin-Tin-Tin's grave.

Radio Flyer (1992)

GSD: Rocky as *Shane*
Trainer: Larry Madrid
Director: Richard Donner
Costars: Elijah Wood, Joseph Mazzello
Country: USA
Status: Available on DVD

Radio Flyer featured a diverse animal cast, including a bison who worked for cookies, a tortoise, many frogs, and a German Shepherd Dog, Rocky—plus his doubles—all from Birds & Animals Unlimited. Much more animal footage was filmed than eventually made it into the final edit. The film, about young brothers and the abuse they suffer at the hands of their stepfather, received poor reviews. From *The New York Times*: "There may have been a good film in David Mickey Evans's screenplay, but it's unrealized by Mr. Donner. . . . Dealing with this delicate material, he is like someone trying to thread a needle while wearing boxing gloves."

Now best known as an early starring role of Elijah Wood's (he was ten years old when the film was made), *Radio Flyer* follows just divorced Mary (Lorraine Bracco) and her two sons, Mikey (Elijah Wood) and Bobby (Joseph Mazzello), as they move west to California with their German Shepherd, Shane (Rocky). They stay with the boys' aunt until Mary meets a man whom Mikey and Bobby call The King (Adam Baldwin) and remarries. They do not tell their mother about The King's rages or his beatings of Bobby.

Only Shane fights back against the reign of terror. Mikey comes up with a plan to save Bobby from The King. They build a flying machine for Bobby with a Radio Flyer wagon at its center. Before, during, and after the construction, Shane is there to fight off bullies, protect their clubhouse, and even make Bobby's escape possible.

When Shane smashes through the screened-in window of the brothers' bedroom to chase away boys breaking into the clubhouse, a soft, nylon-mesh screen was used which tore easily. For his attack scene against The King, the stunt man could not wear hidden padding, because the arm is exposed. A fake arm was made and the dog was taught to bite down on it. Then blood makeup was added to complete the effect.

Call of the Wild (1993)

GSD: Vilas as *Buck*
Trainer: Karl Lewis Miller
Directors: Michael Toshiyuki Uno, Alen Smithee
Costars: Rick Schroder, Gordon Tootoosis
Country: USA
Status: Limited availability

There have been no less than eight live-action features based on *The Call of the Wild*. In some, both Buck and Spitz have been played by GSDs, though the breed was not known at that time and place; 1897 in the Yukon. Buck is even a GSD in the 1981 Japanese animated version. London described a dog that is a Saint Bernard/Rough Collie mix in the novel. In the 1976 version starring John Beck, Burbon, trained by Frank Weatherwax, became the only dog to ever portray Buck appropriately. In the film that is truest to the novel, *The Call of the Wild: Dog of the Yukon* (1996), Buck is a Leonberger, but Spitz is played by a long-haired, sable GSD named Kino.

The first feature-length adaptation, in 1923, had a Saint Bernard in the leading role, and the second, in 1935, was intended to star a German Shepherd. Clark Gable played John Thornton in the film. When he was given a screen test with a Shepherd, it was decided that the dog looked too small next to him, so Buck was again played by a Saint Bernard. While this 1993 made-for-TV adaptation is one of the worst, it hosts the most beautiful German Shepherd to play the role of Buck. Vilas was a classic looking, plush-coated GSD trained by Karl Lewis Miller. He can also be seen in *Chips the War Dog* (see next entry).

This *Call of the Wild* is told through the eyes of John Thornton (Rick Schroder) and his own journal entries. We follow him from his Seattle home to a ship bound for Skagway. Along the journey, Buck (Vilas) is introduced as a subplot. Thornton befriends the dog while still aboard the ship. He tries to buy Buck at auction, but the dog is sold to another bidder while Thornton runs to get his money. The two make their way north separately. Buck's journey does resemble the novel from there: he eventually ends up in the possession of a group of southerners who nearly kill him before his sled team stumbles upon the cabin where Thornton is staying. Thornton rescues Buck and the story continues to wander nonsensically for some time after.

Chips the War Dog (1993)

GSD: Vilas as *Chips*
Trainer: Karl Lewis Miller
Director: Ed Kaplan
Costars: Brandon Douglas, Ned Vaughn
Country: USA
Status: Limited availability

As in his last starring role, here Vilas portrays a dog that was supposed to be a mixed breed. The reason for using a GSD instead lies in both the breed itself—trainability, intelligence, and stamina are all essential for film work—and the same reason purebreds of any kind are generally preferred to mixes for films: it is easier to match a purebred dog with another purebred, so multiple dogs can play a single part.

Chips the War Dog is loosely based on a true story of a famous World War II military dog who would have been difficult to match with a stunt double: Chips was a mix of

Collie, Siberian Husky, and German Shepherd. Chips, who notoriously once bit General Dwight D. Eisenhower, was awarded the Purple Heart and Silver Star after his heroics in the war. They were later withdrawn on the grounds that awarding such things to a dog undermined the medals themselves. After this, U.S. war dogs became classified as "equipment," and no military dog has received a medal since.

Chips (Vilas) is a troublemaker who cannot resist escaping from his family's home to chase chickens on the neighbor's farm. When the family's kids, Jimbo (Luke Rossi) and Peggy (Sheridan Gayr), see a call for volunteers to donate their dogs to Dogs for Defense, they want to help out and also keep Chips out of the pound. Chips is accepted into the program but soon flunks out when he makes no progress in training. Private Danny Stauffer (Brandon Douglas), who is afraid of dogs and never meant to be involved in the program himself, has taken an interest in Chips and secretly keeps the dog at the kennel. Stauffer trains Chips by night and Chips redeems himself when he helps to gain funding for Dogs for Defense. Once Stauffer and Chips are deployed, Chips saves lives as he detects bombs and snipers, runs phone lines to headquarters, takes out pillboxes, and tracks down missing soldiers. Even Rin-Tin-Tin and Thunder would have been proud.

Kazan (1995)

Also known as *Eye of the Wolf*
GSD: Blacky as *Kazan*
Trainer: Raymond Ducasse
Director: Arnaud Sélignac
Costars: Sophie Duez, Jeff Fahey
Countries: Canada, France
Status: Limited availability

During the 1990s, a series of Canadian television movies were coproduced with France: Mostly based on James Oliver Curwood books, as well as Jack London, collectively the six films were known as *Aventures dans le Grand Nord*, or *Adventures of the Great North*. All six have been released on VHS with English titles that often have no relationship to the original French ones. Some are available on DVD, including *Northwest Passage* (1994, PAL format only), which was originally titled *Bari* and was the sequel to *Kazan*, though released before it. *Kazan*, released on VHS as *Eye of the Wolf*, is based on *Kazan: Wolf-Dog of the North*. *Bari* is based on *Baree, son of Kazan*.

Kazan stars a solid black, long-haired German Shepherd. The equally beautiful dog who plays Bari in that film is possibly a long-haired, sable GSD with unusual structure, though he appears to be a Shiloh Shepherd. In both films, along with *The Call of the Wild: Dog of the Yukon*, can be seen some of the most harsh treatment of canines in modern movies. None were monitored by the AHA's Canadian branch. In the latter, a dog is even anesthetized and dragged through the snow by his harness. The training in all three was headed by Raymond Ducasse of Pro-Film Animal, Inc.

The story follows Kazan (Blacky) as he witnesses the murder of his master and is almost shot himself for his savagery before Jo (Sophie Duez) rushes to save him. She is warned by a zoologist, Paul (Jeff Fahey), that the dog is part wolf, but Jo does not care. Years pass as Kazan moves back and forth from a domesticated life with Jo to roaming the wilderness. When his mate is blinded by a cougar, he acts as her guide. Then Taggart (Lorne Brass), one of the men who killed his master, reenters Kazan's life, brutally abusing him and taking him to a fighting ring. There, Paul finds Kazan and tells Taggart he will fight him for the dog. Real dead animals are shown in *Kazan*, including a duck, pheasant, rabbit, and cougar. There is a startling canine fight scene, and more alarming are the tripwires used on dogs running at full speed, similar to those used in the 1972 GSD spaghetti western, *Cry of the Black Wolves*.

Bad Moon (1996)

GSD: Primo as *Thor*
Trainer: Mark Dumas
Director: Eric Red
Costars: Mariel Hemingway, Michael Paré
Country: USA
Status: Available on DVD

Primo belonged to Mark Dumas of Creative Animal Talent in British Columbia, Canada. Dumas specializes in wild and exotic animals for film and worked for several years at Steve Martin's Working Wildlife in Southern California. Primo had many film and TV appearances throughout his long career. Soon after his starring role in *Bad Moon*, he was the villain in *Dogboys* (see page 168). In 2000, he played Spitz for yet another version of *The Call of the Wild*, this time in the form of a short-lived Animal Planet TV series. In his senior years, he can be seen as Yoko in *National Lampoon's Holiday Reunion* (2003). By then, he had grown fat and sassy and is nearly unrecognizable compared to the athletic dog seen in *Bad Moon*.

Bad Moon is based on Wayne Smith's novel, *Thor*, which is told mostly from the dog's point of view. The trailer for the film downplays Thor's part in it so much that only a glimpse of him is caught at all, though the action really revolves around him. Janet (Mariel Hemingway) invites her brother Ted (Michael Paré) to stay on her property in his little RV after bodies are found in the wilderness nearby. Thor (Primo) discovers Ted's secret when he tracks him through the woods one night and finds a werewolf in his place. Thor won't let Ted out of his sight after that, day or night. While Janet and Brett (Mason Gamble), her son, remain unaware of Ted's nightly transformations, Thor is on guard and ready to protect his family.

Primo's repertoire included doing bite work, but when it came time to tackle the nearly eight-foot-tall werewolf, a pro was brought in: Fina z Poluxu CS, or Fina, a black and tan female belonging to Tony and Katie Nikl of Canczech Kennels near Vancouver, B.C., doubled for the attacks. She did this so well that stuntman Ken Kirzinger, in the werewolf suite, asked to use the on-hand prosthetic dog for some of the final scenes—that dog did not bite back.

Buck and the Magic Bracelet (1997)

Also known as *Buck e il braccialetto magico*

GSD: *Buck*

Trainer: Sebastiano Arcifa

Director: Tonino Ricci

Costars: Matt McCoy, Abby Dalton

Countries: Italy, USA

Status: Limited availability

Buck is credited as playing himself in this film, though that seems an unlikely name for an Italian dog. The Shepherd was trained by veteran GSD trainer Sebastiano Arcifa, who was responsible for the Italian *White Fang* films. Arcifa owned a kennel: La Scuola Dei Campioni, or "The School of Champions." The kennel is still being run today by Angelo Arcifa, who trains performance German Shepherds for protection and obedience, as well as agility and film work.

The sequel to *Buck at the Edge of Heaven* (1991), *Buck and the Magic Bracelet* is a relatively modern spaghetti western that is often mistakenly credited as being from 1999. It is a co-production between Italy's Gruppo Minerva company and PM Entertainment Group of the United States. PM's films are now owned by Echo Bridge Home Entertainment, which has never released the film. It can be seen on VHS and received a limited PAL DVD release. However, it is best to avoid this travesty of filmmaking. Though it reportedly cost $1.5 million to make, that sum apparently could not cover decent cameras or film, a competent cinematographer, or actors who did not woodenly repeat every line without changing expressions. The dog, who appears to be a black and tan except in close-ups, when he looks like a liver and tan, is the most capable actor.

A teenage boy named Kevin (Frankie Nero) lives with his German Shepherd, Buck, and his father, Zan (Bruno Minniti, credited as Conrad Nichols), at a Canadian mining camp. A group of Bible-toting murderers and thieves is on the loose who ride into camp one day, kill the other men, wound Kevin and Zan, and dognap Buck. With the help of Natty (Matt McCoy), a friend of his father's, and the impostor native shaman Shanka (Felton Perry), Kevin sets out to search for both Buck and his missing father. Although the story would not appeal to anyone over the age of six or seven, *Buck and the Magic Bracelet* is PG-13 and riddled with incessant and unnecessary violence and swearing.

Baby Rex (1997)

Also known as *Baby Rex - Der kleine Kommissar*
GSD: *Rex*
Trainer: Teresa Ann Miller
Director: Oliver Hirschbiegel
Costars: Friedrich von Thun, Christine Neubauer
Country: Austria
Status: Available on DVD (PAL format only)

In 1993, Teresa Ann Miller and her father, Karl Lewis Miller, began training on an Austrian television show that would end up becoming one of the most popular dog series ever produced. Known around the world and released from Finland to Canada, Australia, Brazil, Vietnam, and over forty other countries, *Kommissar Rex*, or *Inspector Rex*, has run for so long that the show is on its fourth leading man, all of whom teamed up with Rex as his police sidekick. The show is now being produced in Italy in its ninth season, with Kaspar Capparoni in the costarring role beside the dog.

Baby Rex (the literal title translation is *Baby Rex - The Little Inspector*) is the TV movie which charts Rex's early beginnings, before he joined the police force. In the film, Rex, born from a famed champion line, is stolen as a puppy. He escapes his captors and makes his way in the snow to a young boy, Benny (Raphael Ghobadloo), who needs Rex as much as the puppy needs him. Rex's rightful owners come to claim him, but Rex does not want to leave Benny, whose father recently died. Many months later, Benny and Rex find themselves mixed up in criminal activity as they track down bad guys together.

Besides the variety of adult, red and black German Shepherds playing in the series—notably Reginald von Ravenhorst—Teresa Ann Miller, along with Karl Lewis Miller, April Morley, Melinda Eichberg, and Cathy McCallum, had to train a group of puppies for the film. Rex goes from about eight weeks old through about eight months in the film. The young dogs in *Baby Rex* do some extraordinary things for their age, mastering complex actions and long shots with apparent ease. The show was such a hit that Teresa Ann Miller wrote a book (in German only) called *Hundetraining mit Kommissar Rex* (*Dog Training with Inspector Rex*). Though mostly pictorial, it features training tips and credits Miller as a "Hollywood-Startrainerin."

Fina rehearses for one of her attack scenes with her trainer, Tony Nikl, as stuntman on the set of *Dogboys*. (Courtesy Tony Nikl, photo by Katie Nikl)

Dogboys (1998)

Also known as *Tracked*

GSD: Primo as *Clyde*

Trainer: Mark Dumas

Director: Ken Russell

Costars: Dean Cain, Bryan Brown

Country: Canada

Status: Available on DVD

After Fina's spectacular performance in *Bad Moon* (see page 162), Tony and Katie Nikl continued working with their German Shepherds in films and provided most of the dogs in *Dogboys* who appeared alongside Mark Dumas's Primo in the starring role. The made-for-TV film, retitled *Tracked* for its VHS release, was originally scripted with intense dog attack scenes throughout, but it was watered down to a drama rather than a thriller during production. Primo and the other dogs, mostly German Shepherds, including Fina, still get a decent amount of screen time in the edited film.

When Julian Taylor (Dean Cain), an ex-Marine, lands in prison for aggravated assault, he quickly finds himself in trouble for fighting with another con and lands in the dog-house, literally. Taylor is sent to a group of inmates known as dogboys. They take care of the prison dogs and run tracks to train the dogs to hunt down escapees. Taylor reluctantly begins to befriend another convict, Willy B. (Richard Chevolleau), who shows him the ropes with the dogs. Unknown to Taylor, Willy is an undercover cop who is investigating the guard in charge of the dog unit, Captain Robert Brown (Bryan Brown), for money laundering. After Captain Brown's dog, Clyde (Primo), kills Willy in the kennels one night, Taylor becomes part of the investigation with the prompting of Deputy D.A. Jennifer Dern (Tia Carrere)—only now the investigation is for murder.

Dean Cain did some of his own stunt work with the dogs, being attacked by both Primo and Fina, who does the first takedown in the film, coming in like a train. For the stunt work late in the film Tony Nikl doubled for Bryan Brown so Fina could attack his leg while he hung onto a fence. Other German Shepherds from Canczech Kennels to appear in movies include Ice, the sable dog locating men inside boxes in *Dogboys*, as well as Dusty, Dallas, Troy, Roland, Solo, and Bobi. Just a few of their roles are in *Garden State* (2004), *The Pink Panther* (2006), *Watchmen* (2009), *2012* (2009), the TV miniseries *Intensity* (1997), and several others. Their biggest role was for *Ace of Hearts* (see page 198).

Atomic Dog (1998)

GSD: *Cerberus*
Trainer: Roger Schumacher
Director: Brian Trenchard-Smith
Costars: Daniel Hugh Kelly, Isabella Hofmann
Country: USA
Status: Limited availability

A U.S. made-for-TV production filmed in Alberta, Canada, this film never decided what it wanted to be when it grew up. Billed as a thriller, *Atomic Dog* is essentially a children's movie that is too violent for very young kids. The large canine cast, provided by Birds & Animals Unlimited and a team of trainers including Roger Schumacher, Stacey Basil, Ray Beal, and Cheryl Harris, features a white German Shepherd, a Golden Retriever, and two large mixed breeds, one of which also starred in the Disney Channel movie, *You Lucky Dog* (1998).

The Devil's Canyon Nuclear Power Plant is closed down after a leak, but someone is left behind: Cerberus is a puppy who grows up alone at the plant. When the Yates family moves into town, Josh (Micah Gardener) finds himself at the plant with three other teenage boys, who spot a strange dog through the fence and start taking shots at him. Josh, who is accompanied by his sister's dog, Trixie, leaves in disgust. The next day, Trixie is missing, and one of the boys is found dead. Cerberus has stolen Trixie away to be his mate, but she returns to her home two months later, where she dies after giving birth to two puppies. Josh and his sister, Heather (Katie Stuart), adopt the pups, Lobo and Scamp. But once the pups are grown up, Cerberus returns for them, and he does not mind killing the humans in his way to get what he wants.

Cerberus was dyed black along his back and down his shoulders and hips so he did not appear to be just another German Shepherd. No protection dogs were used in the film, and the actor dogs did their own stunts, leaping for concealed toys in the clothing of the actors and trainer/stuntmen to achieve the attack scenes. The plastic snarl device is also used for the film. Although *Atomic Dog* is the last film profiled in this book to star a white German Shepherd, there are certainly other modern releases to feature these beautiful dogs, such as *Amos and Andrew* (1993) and *Getting Away with Murder* (1996).

A Dog's Tale (1999)

GSD: Casey as *Tim*
Trainer: Shawn Hayes
Director: Craig Clyde
Costars: Gordon Jump, Clayton Taylor
Country: USA
Status: Available on DVD

A Dog's Tale was a straight-to-DVD family film from writer/director/producer team Craig Clyde and Bryce Fillmore, responsible for several other independent animal movies, including *Little Heroes* (1992), *Castle Rock* (2000), and *Miracle Dogs* (2003)—the first about a girl and her German Shepherd mix, and the second another German Shepherd film. Casey, the black and tan female German Shepherd in *A Dog's Tale* was a rescue dog who started police work before getting the starring role for the film. Casey even gets her name in the opening credits.

Tim (Clayton Taylor) wants a dog for Christmas more than anything else, but his parents have forbidden it. When Tim meets eccentric Thaddeus Widstoe (Gordon Jump), who refers to himself as the Professor, he is drawn in by a tale of the Christmas star and makes a wish on the star. The wish comes true but goes terribly wrong: instead of getting a dog, Tim becomes a dog (Casey). Now he's on a mission to find the Professor, somehow communicate what has happened, and see if anything can be done to get him back to normal.

Along the way, he faces angry neighbors, wolves, a bear, and the police.

Principle photography was done in Utah, with additional outdoor footage shot in Idaho and Montana. The wild animals, including a pack of gray wolves, a lynx, a fisher, a raccoon, a skunk, and a bear, were filmed on their own turf at Animals of Montana, Inc. Trainer Troy Hyde used a buzzer to call the wolf pack from point A to point B and make it appear that the wolves were chasing Casey, though the dog was never in the same scene with the pack and only appeared in a brief scene with one of the wolves. In this scene, a Golden Retriever named Bear played the part of Tim's friend, who fights off the wolf and saves him from attack. Bear had been raised at the Montana game farm, and the wolf pack thought of him as the alpha, so his tussle with the omega wolf for the shot was nothing special to Bear.

K-911 (1999)

GSD: Mac as *Jerry Lee*
Trainer: April Morley
Director: Charles T. Kanganis
Costars: James Belushi, Christine Tucci
Country: USA
Status: Available on DVD

April Morley was head trainer, through Karl Lewis Miller's company, Animal Action, for this ten-year-later sequel to *K-9* (see page 148) Other trainers for the film included Alvin Mears and Cathy McCallum, who worked with Teresa Ann Miller and April Morley in Austria on *Kommissar Rex*.

Detective Dooley (James Belushi)—whose first name in *K-9* is Michael, but abruptly becomes Thomas for the next two films—and his K-9 partner are nearing their retirement years and doing nothing more thrilling than visiting the ATM when an armored gunman tries to kill Dooley. Jerry Lee (Mac) takes off in pursuit when the man runs, and Dooley follows behind. But the would-be assassin makes his escape over a fence and onto a motorcycle after a harrowing chase, leaving both Dooley and Jerry Lee gasping for breath. After the failed chase, the two are assigned new partners in the form of Sergeant Welles (Christine Tucci) and her rigidly disciplined, hyper-responsive Doberman Pinscher, Zeus (Lucan). Welles and Zeus are no more pleased by the pairing than Dooley and Jerry Lee are, but a grudging respect develops as they move ever closer to solving the case.

Mac has similar structure to Rando, though stockier, and seems a pretty close match to what an aged Jerry Lee would look like. There is a nod to one of Miller's most successful dog films, *Beethoven*, when Dooley tells Jerry Lee he'll play the movie for him while he, Dooley, leaves the house. Mac is given an opening credit in *K-911* after the humans are listed. His doubles for the film were Sonto, Reno, and King. In one scene, Belushi uses Mac's real name. This was possibly scripted, since *mac* could be generic usage, like *pal* or *buddy*, or it could be a mistake not caught in post-production.

A home portrait of Asko, one of the stars of *Wilderness* (2006).
(Courtesy Helmut Lüking, photo by Helmut Lüking)

Still Heroes: The 2000s

After nine decades of German Shepherd movie stars, the breed is still going strong as a favorite of the big screen with such recent films as *I Am Legend* (2007) and *Beverly Hills Chihuahua* (2008). The films are more complex, more expensive, and more involved. But the dog is still the dog. Still the heart and soul of a film. Still a hero and a friend, with no more or less power to captivate an audience than when Strongheart first flickered across the silver screen. And, after so many years, still one of the top dogs in Hollywood and in films around the world.

Bear and the cast of *Bring Him Home*. From left, Sharon Gless, Edward Asner, and Jeffrey Licon. (Courtesy Rob Bloch, photo by Rob Bloch)

Bring Him Home (2000)

GSD: Bear as *Buddy*

Trainer: Rob Bloch

Director: Robert Fedor

Costars: Jeffrey Licon, Edward Asner

Country: USA

Status: Available on DVD

Writer/director Robert Fedor seems to have been unable to decide on one type of story for this straight-to-DVD independent film. Instead he threw several ideas together—racism, experimentation on animals, corrupt justice systems, alcoholism, immigrants, pet theft, grandpar-ents/children, among them—until the resulting film is so annoying and slow-moving that it is difficult to watch. The only thing that makes *Bring Him Home* worth seeing is the gorgeous, black and tan, long-haired German Shepherd named Bear. The dog scenes in the film were shot in only six days. The Los Angeles Animal Shelter, along with the trainer's own kennel facility, served as sets.

Bear was found on the streets of Palmdale, California, by a trainer from the Lake Hughes–based company, Critters of the Cinema. When no owner was located, he became a part of the Critters team headed by Rob Bloch. Bear appeared in several TV shows, including *Sunset Beach* in 1999 and *CSI: Crime Scene Investigation* in 2001. He also did commercials, along with one other independent feature, *The Trouble with Lou* (2001), a satire in which he plays a guard dog wearing a Nazi armband. Bear retired two years after doing *Bring Him Home*.

Bring Him Home starts out as a boy-and-his-dog film until Ricky (Jeffrey Licon) steals a can of dog food for his German Shepherd, Buddy (Bear). The sleazy Cadie Murkison (Noah Blake), who tried to buy Buddy from Ricky and was refused, sees him slip the can under his sweatshirt and stops him at the door. After Ricky makes a run for it, he is caught by the police. Buddy is taken to the animal shelter with the understanding that the boy will be back for him, and he is not seen much thereafter. The dog is stolen from the shelter by Cadie, with help from a shelter worker who is in on Cadie's gig of selling stolen animals for medical research. To Ricky's own surprise, he finds help getting his dog back from his alienated grandfather (Edward Asner).

Rain (2001)

GSD: *Rain*

Trainer: Karl Lewis Miller

Director: Robert J. Wilson

Costars: Scott Cooper, Pamela Moore Somers

Country: USA

Status: Available on DVD (PAL format only)

Rain is a made-for-TV, Animal Planet Original Movie about a Vietnam War dog. It was later released on DVD in Europe but has never been commercially available in any format in the United States or Canada. It first aired in 2001, a year in which three other films with the exact same title were released.

Rain is a German Shepherd who is volunteered by his family and travels to Vietnam with handler Private Holland (Scott Cooper) but is greeted with open skepticism by the rest of his platoon. Both dog and handler must prove themselves before the other men can learn to trust them. Rain has an even greater difficulty to overcome: a crippling fear of water. The dog performs wonderfully throughout the film, but the same cannot be said for the human actors. The film is disappointingly clichéd and historically inaccurate.

Decades after Chips had his medals taken away from him and all U.S. war dogs were classified as equipment, a documentary was released about the fate of those dogs who had to live, and die, with that classification: *War Dogs: America's Forgotten Heroes* (1999), with dramatized sequences featuring dogs trained by Karl Lewis Miller, tells their story.

Rain tells a fictionalized account of one of these dogs which sugarcoats the real one. About 4,000 U.S. military dogs served in the Vietnam War. Almost all were German Shepherds. They saved thousands of human lives, and many gave their own lives to do so. When the war was over, the U.S. military refused to bring them home. Far from being decorated, these war heroes were either euthanized or handed over to the South Vietnamese army. It is unknown if any were actually smuggled out alive by their handlers, as depicted in *Rain*. U.S. military dogs would continue to be classified as equipment until a bill passed in 2000, which allowed these dogs to be retired and adopted.

K-9: P.I. (2002)

GSD: King as *Jerry Lee*
Trainer: Karl Lewis Miller
Director: Richard J. Lewis
Costars: James Belushi, Kim Huffman
Country: USA
Status: Available on DVD

The first *K-9* sequel was a tolerable, if idiotic, attempt at exploiting a slightly name-recognized film for all it was worth. This third *K-9* film is even worse than the second and a thorough waste of time and money. Where Mac was a credible imitation of an older Rando, King, who plays Jerry Lee here, is a heavily built, black and red dog with a broad skull and muzzle. King performed some stunts for Mac in the second film but does not fit well as the lead, although James Belushi praised him as being the best dog to work with in any of the films and was himself inspired to get two GSD puppies after working on the *K-9* movies.

In this film, Dooley (James Belushi) and Jerry Lee (King) have just entered retirement when they become involved in a murder/theft case, and Dooley's pension is put on hold while the FBI investigates. But the thieves do not get away with what they tried to take—a computer chip of the future. Jerry Lee swallows it. In an effort to gain some income for himself and his dog, Dooley puts out an ad as a private investigator and offers Jerry Lee up as a stud dog. A breeder (Jody Racicot) introduces them to several dogs, including a Dachshund, in a scene reminiscent of Pongo's watching out the window of his London flat for a mate in the animated *101 Dalmatians* (1961). Dooley gets an answer to his P.I. ad in the form of a beautiful woman (Kim Huffman). She tells Dooley her fiancé is missing, but Dooley soon begins to unravel her connection to the case that has caused his pension to be suspended.

Teresa Ann Miller trained alongside her father on *K-9: P.I.* King shared his role with three doubles: Ponya, Sontal, and Ace. Dooley takes center stage in this one, while Jerry Lee provides the only amusing moments, sitting on top of the refrigerator, and later shredding a seat in Dooley's car in an effort to reach a cell phone which Dooley tried to teach him to dial with a pencil. In a scene where Dooley pours a beer for his dog, King was really drinking apple juice.

Scent of Danger (2002)

Also known as *Scent of Murder*

GSD: Iago as *Brie*

Trainer: Josée Juteau

Director: Peter Svatek

Costars: Sherilyn Fenn, Costas Mandylor

Country: Canada

Status: Available on DVD

On the heels of *Rain*, *Scent of Danger* was another Animal Planet Original Movie. It aired on October 23, 2002. It was based on the novel *Scent of Murder*, by Cynthia G. Alwyn, and the title was changed to that of the book for the DVD release. Filmed in Montreal, though set in Boston, the dogs were provided by Raymond Ducasse's Pro-Film Animal, Inc., with Josée Juteau as head trainer.

Brenna (Sherilyn Fenn) is a seasoned search and rescue dog handler with her highly trained German Shepherd, Brie (Iago), by her side. When the two are called in one night to the case of a missing child, Brenna has no idea her life is about to be turned upside-down. She and Brie corner the kidnapper (James McGowan) on a bridge over a river. Brenna is powerless to stop him from dropping Zoe (Alicia Ducasse) over the side, but Brie charges in after her and saves the little girl's life. In the days to follow, Brenna realizes she and her dogs have become the new target for the kidnapper. He begins stalking her, first sending a string of emails, then breaking into her home. His next target is Brie, and Brenna must turn to her unruly novice dog, an Australian Shepherd named Feather (Nixon), to track him down.

In Alwyn's novel, Brie, a female German Shepherd, is swept away and killed in the river while saving Zoe right at the beginning of the book. Brie, played in the film by Iago, a black and tan male, is a much more central character here. Brenna's other dog, Feather, is a Bouvier de Flanders in the book. The change to a blue merle Australian Shepherd may have been a choice of either the director, for reasons of visibility on screen, since black and very dark dogs are seldom used in starring roles, or of the trainer, if an Aussie was the best dog at hand for the job.

The Breed (2006)

GSD: Several
Trainer: Paul "Sled" Reynolds
Director: Nicholas Mastandrea
Costars: Michelle Rodriguez, Oliver Hudson
Countries: Germany, South Africa, USA
Status: Available on DVD

Although this film was promoted as *Wes Craven's The Breed*, Wes Craven neither wrote, produced, nor directed it. He was the executive producer, which essentially means he assisted in financing but did not necessarily have anything more to do with it.

A group of five young men and women go on vacation to an isolated island retreat that was inherited by the two brothers of the film (Oliver Hudson and Eric Lively) from their uncle. What starts as an endless swimming and drinking party ends as a desperate fight for life after the other inhabitants on the island show themselves; a pack of twenty-nine dogs who were genetically modified by military scientists. The dogs chew through the rope of the group's float plane on the dock, crash through windows, stalk them in the woods, climb onto roofs, and leap straight into the air in an effort to grab heroine Nikki (Michelle Rodriguez) off a zipline.

Some of the most unusual and realistic attack scenes ever filmed in a dog movie can be seen in *The Breed*, often with multiple dogs. The pack in the film is about half German Shepherds, with a large variety within the breed: short- and long-haired in several colors. The real names of the GSDs include Mister, Jessie, and Enzo. Black GSD Enzo—a native of South Africa, where the film was made, and trained by Ryan Leach—had to do a difficult leg-bite scene in which he twice missed his mark of a hidden pad and bit first the stunt double, then actress Michelle Rodriguez, on the leg.

The dogs were made up of both movie and protection dogs brought from Los Angeles by Sled Reynolds and his company, Gentle Jungle Animals, and protection dogs from

South Africa with head trainer Gavin Van Munster. Ten trainers in all, including Thomas Roach and Tamara Andrews, worked on the film. Other breeds seen in the movie are a Dutch Shepherd named Hank; three Belgian Malinois brothers named Bullet, Brownie, and Neo; a Rottweiler; and mixed breeds.

Wilderness (2006)

GSD: Several
Trainer: Dorothee Lüking
Director: Michael J. Bassett
Costars: Sean Pertwee, Alex Reid
Country: UK
Status: Available on DVD

Do not be deceived by this DVD's cover, which shows a Belgian Malinois, a Doberman Pinscher, a mixed breed, and what appears to be an African wild dog. Not one of these animals can be seen in *Wilderness*, which takes story ideas from several other films. It bears some resemblance to *The Breed*, which was released the same year by the same company, First Look Studios. What *Wilderness* does feature is a pack of four sable and black and tan German Shepherds who are killing machines trained to a whistle like sheepdogs. The dogs are played by Angie, Asko, Dusty, and Skipper.

The GSDs on the set of *Wilderness* (Skipper, Asko, Dusty, and Angie) demonstrate how actors spend much of their time at work: waiting. (Courtesy Helmut Lüking, photo by Helmut Lüking)

A group of young male convicts is sent to a remote island as punishment and for a character-building exercise after they refuse to own up to having tormented another convict until he committed suicide. Shortly after arriving at the uninhabited island, they discover they are not alone after all; the area has been double booked with female prisoners, there's a strange hermit in the woods, and someone is trying to kill them with a crossbow and four trained dogs. The German Shepherd pack tracks and corners them at every turn, attacking viciously and only letting up the pursuit when commanded by the whistle. But after their supervising officers (Sean Pertwee and Alex Reid) are killed, a greater threat to the young men and women than the man hunting them or the dogs tracking them is each other.

The film was shot in Scotland and Ireland with dogs trained by Schutzhund trainer Dorothee Lüking of Scotland, along with her husband, Helmut Lüking, who has trained for the Central Scotland Police. On the UK team, Dorothee Lüking has competed with her German Shepherd Dogs in the Schutzhund World Championships three different years.

The Hills Have Eyes (2006)

GSD: *Beast*

Trainer: Lmahjoub Boulmi

Director: Alexandre Aja

Costars: Aaron Stanford, Kathleen Quinlan

Country: USA

Status: Available on DVD

For this remake of *The Hills Have Eyes*, the two German Shepherds are back to protect their family from horrors in the hills, though playing a much smaller role than in the first film. This one was filmed in Morocco, and only two German Shepherds, who came from France, were provided for the production. Where multiple dogs served as stunt doubles in the original, these Shepherds were expected to perform repeated takes at 120°F and above in the Moroccan desert. The AHA was not contacted to monitor the extensive animal sequences, which include not only the two dogs, but lizards, scorpions, a pig, and several birds. Though most, including the dogs, appear to be well cared for, the birds all look as though they are on their last legs, and the dogs frequently look as though they are near overheating.

Once again, a family is on a road trip to California through the desert. Their tires blow out, and they do not realize it was no accident. Big Bob (Ted Levine) and his son-in-law, Doug (Aaron Stanford), set out to find help. Soon after, they are attacked by people suffering from nuclear radiation who live in the hills. The family's female German Shepherd, Beauty, is the first to fall victim to them, followed by Big Bob. After several horrific encounters, Doug sets out to find his infant daughter, who has been taken by the hill people. This is where the major difference between the original and the remake comes in: Doug discovers a dilapidated town where the killers live and finds himself fighting for his life and his child. Beast accompanies him, once saving his life.

Only one scene employs a dog double, and it is one of the last in the film. Beast was required to show his teeth and snarl right before an implied attack scene. The main dog would not do it and the director had to call in a police dog from Casablanca. This dog performed the scene perfectly.

Devil Dog (2007)

GSD: Yarbo as *Cory*

Trainer: Kerry Foster

Director: Catherine Glover

Costars: Stefanie Hubbard, Brad Crates

Country: USA

Status: Limited availability

The production values on *Devil Dog* are about the same as the average home video of your kids learning to ride their bikes. Yet the budget did allow for a DVD release, including distribution on Amazon.com, for a brief time before being discontinued. The only character in the film whose every line is not exposition is Yarbo the dog, making *Devil Dog* most enjoyable to view with the sound off. The best thing about this film is the cover art for the DVD, which leads us to believe it is about a terrifying dog from hell.

It cannot even be said that the dog puts in a good performance here: Yarbo makes a great Cory, who is the pet German Shepherd of a little girl named Lacy (Hayley Thompson). He appears to be very patient and gentle with the girl, the quintessential family pet. But Yarbo also has to play a rabid dog who wanders aimlessly, attacking people in a small town. He remains gentle and low-key for these scenes as well. The story revolves around Lacy being adopted through a kind of child black market after her parents are killed in a house fire (Lacy and both parents are sound asleep in the middle of the day when this happens). Her adoptive parents, Sara (Stefanie Hubbard) and Taylor (Brad Crates), take in Lacy's dog, Cory, as well. One night, Cory gets into a fight with a skunk, then vanishes the next day. After this, the killer dog appears, whom everyone thinks is Cory.

In real life, Yarbo was a search and rescue dog based in Shreveport, Louisiana. His handler, Kerry Foster, founded the Shreveport Fire Department Search and Rescue Task Force, which has worked over 150 jobs in Louisiana, Texas, Arkansas, and South Carolina. Yarbo was noted for many successful searches, working as both a trailer and cadaver dog. In August 2000, at the age of three, he found the body of a man who had been missing for over a month.

Finding Rin Tin Tin (2007)

Also know as *Rintintin*
GSD: Marco as *Rin Tin Tin*
Trainer: Dimitar Shopov
Director: Danny Lerner
Costars: Tyler Jensen, Gregory Gudgeon
Countries: Bulgaria, USA
Status: Available on DVD

In 1976, Herbert Leonard, producer of the TV shows *The Adventures of Rin Tin Tin* and *Rin Tin Tin: K-9 Cop*, sued Paramount Pictures for copyright infringement from *Won Ton*

Ton, the Dog Who Saved Hollywood (see page 128). Thirty-two years later, Daphne Hereford, owner of the Rin Tin Tin trademark and breeding stock descended from Rin-Tin-Tin, sued First Look Studios, Inc., and its affiliates, over *Finding Rin Tin Tin*. The film had been released theatrically in France as *Rintintin* in 2007, with a huge amount of publicity, but it did not arrive in the United States until 2008.

Where *Won Ton Ton* was a spoof film, only hinting at its relationship to Rin Tin Tin, *Finding Rin Tin Tin* actually claims to be based on the true story of the original Rin-Tin-Tin. A reasonable comparison would be a company releasing a movie about an Alaskan Eskimo who takes up playing the guitar in the 1950s and saying it is based on the true story of Elvis. Unsatisfied with making up a story and claiming it was connected to the original Rin-Tin-Tin, the filmmakers took the extra step of going out of their way to portray the dog in every disgusting and ludicrous situation they could come up with, from getting drunk to urinating into a man's mug when his back is turned, after which the man drinks from the mug.

The movie included cast and crew from Bulgaria (where it was filmed), the United States, the Czech Republic, the UK, and others. The German Shepherds came from Lary Mak Kennels in Sofia, Bulgaria, owned by Dimitar Shopov, as well as a Czech Republic company called Fauna & Film. The plot follows a German Shepherd puppy from being found in a bombed French town during World War I to working as a search and rescue dog in adulthood. Along the way, the dog flies in military aircraft, salutes with an artificial limb, drops eggs on men's heads, continually awakens soldiers in the barracks he sleeps in, and involves himself in a poker game. Eleven dogs were used to play the role from pup to adult, including Marco, Oskar, Sunny, Mira, Zuzi, Lana, and Andy.

I Am Legend (2007)

GSD: Abbey as *Samantha*
Trainer: Steve Berens
Director: Francis Lawrence
Costars: Will Smith, Alice Braga
Country: USA
Status: Available on DVD

Based on the sci-fi/horror novel by Richard Matheson, and a remake of two different films, *The Last Man on Earth* (1964) and *The Omega Man* (1971), *I Am Legend* is the first version of the story to star a German Shepherd Dog. And what better companion when you're alone in the world?

Will Smith plays Dr. Robert Neville, a researcher and sole survivor living in New York City after a miracle cure for cancer mutated and killed almost the entire population of the world. By his side in his day to day struggle to maintain sanity in his isolation; to discover a cure for the diseased, zombie-like people roaming the streets by night; and just to stay alive, is his three-year-old German Shepherd, Sam (Abbey). With the exception of a group of mannequins residing at the local movie rental store, Neville has only his dog to talk to, and Sam listens, demonstrating one of the best, most natural performances of a German Shepherd in modern film, and, of course, saving his life along the way.

Abbey was adopted from a California kennel by trainer Steve Berens of Animals of Distinction, Inc. She had the light coloring that the director was looking for, but she did not even know basic obedience or her own name. Berens had only three weeks to prep Abbey before she met Will Smith for the first time and headed to New York for the six-month shoot. Abbey spent time bonding with Smith before filming, and he became so attached to the dog that he asked Berens if he could keep her, telling him to name a price. But Berens would not sell.

Abbey attended The Genesis Awards in 2008, where she posed with Wayne Pacelle, president and CEO of The Humane Society of the United States. A prequel to *I Am Legend* is upcoming, though it is doubtful Abbey will be seen in it.

Underdog (2007)

GSD: Several

Trainer: William S. Grisco

Director: Frederik Du Chau

Costars: Peter Dinklage, James Belushi

Country: USA

Status: Available on DVD

Underdog was originally a 1960s animated television series about a Beagle called Shoeshine Boy. He had an alter ego as the crime-fighting superhero, Underdog. In 2007, Walt Disney released a live-action film based on the series which utilizes a combination of real dogs and CGI to create the talking, flying, super dogs in the film. First seen as a team of police dogs, and later fighting for the bad guys, is a trio of German Shepherds—called Kill, Attack, and Maim, and played by Rocket, among others—who get the same genetic modification treatment that Shoeshine does. Though the GSDs are not the top dogs of the film, *Underdog* was the first movie to work with German Shepherds as major live-action/CGI characters, not only making them talk but also giving them incredible strength and the ability to fly.

A young Beagle (played by Huey and Leo and voiced by Jason Lee) is a bomb-sniffing dog who loses his job when he alerts to a hambone instead of an explosive. He ends up in the laboratory of evil Dr. Barsinister (Peter Dinklage), but escapes, running into a case of the mad doctor's experiments on the way and becoming covered in strange liquids. Back on the street, he is hit by a car, then taken home by its driver, Dan (James Belushi). Dan names him Shoeshine for his interest in licking shoes and tries to get his son, Jack (Alex Neuberger), to make friends with the dog. It's not until Shoeshine realizes what has happened to him and Jack realizes the dog can talk to him, that the two set out to make Shoeshine into the heroic Underdog.

One of the most demanding shots for the German Shepherds comes late in *Underdog*, when all three had to stay in formation for a long shot. The scene was cut from the film but can be viewed in the deleted scenes feature of the DVD. Each dog worked with his own trainer on set from Boone's Animals for Hollywood, Inc., which provided many of the animals for another talking Beagle film, *Cats and Dogs* (2001).

Solo takes a dive off of a pier for a scene at the beginning of *Ace of Hearts*. (Courtesy Tony Nikl, photo by Katie Nikl)

Ace of Hearts (2008)

GSD: Solo as *Ace*
Trainer: Tony Nikl
Director: David Mackay
Costars: Dean Cain, Britt McKillip
Countries: Canada, USA
Status: Available on DVD

Ace of Hearts is based on a true story about a police dog which first appeared in *Reader's Digest*. Tony Nikl was contacted to provide the dog for the title role but waited in vain for any news on dates.

A year later, Nikl found out the film was going forward, but he now had only one dog appropriate to play the demanding role of Ace: Canczech's Solo (the only puppy of his litter) was a six-year-old, 120-pound, black and tan male who had appeared alongside Steve Martin in *The Pink Panther* as an airport security dog. The Nikls had a one-year-old, sable female who was going into advanced training and doing well. Bobi could double, if only she looked anything like Solo. Sandy Moore, C.M.G., owner of Animal Haven Grooming in British Columbia, spent two weeks perfecting a color job on Bobi until Solo had a double so convincing that members of the crew did not notice when Nikl switched dogs back and forth on the set.

Solo, who appears on the cover of this book, is a third-generation star: his mother, Troy, was the German Shepherd of the sled team in *Kevin of the North* (2001), also called *Chilly*

Dogs, and his grandmother, Fina, was the Nikls' first movie dog. Bobi's father, Roland, a veteran of film and TV work, has a brief appearance in *Ace of Hearts* as a snarling potential police dog. Solo and Bobi were later teamed up together for a minor role in a major film when they appeared as the bloodthirsty dogs of a murderer in *Watchmen*.

Ace (Solo) works with Officer Daniel Harding (Dean Cain) and comes first in Harding's life over his wife, Lilly (Anne Marie DeLuise), and his thirteen-year-old daughter, Julia (Britt McKillip). Ace and Harding are on the trail of a notorious burglar when Ace gets ahead of his handler and corners the man, Torko (Mike Dopud, also a stuntman). By the time Harding and his backup reach Ace, Torko is screaming in pain, and there are gashes on his throat. Ace is believed responsible and is sent to an out-of-town clinic to be put down. He makes a break for it while Julia is trying to solve his case and prove his innocence back home.

Solo, right, with Bobi, who was dyed to match him for *Ace of Hearts*. (Photo by Jordan Taylor)

Beverly Hills Chihuahua (2008)

GSD: Samson as *Delgado*
Trainer: Ray Beal
Director: Raja Gosnell
Costars: Piper Perabo, Manolo Cardona
Country: USA
Status: Available on DVD

Contrary to the title, *Beverly Hills Chihuahua* is mostly about a German Shepherd who plays a much larger role than the dog featured in the center of the DVD cover. The team from Birds & Animals Unlimited is no stranger to challenging films, yet *Beverly Hills Chihuahua* seems to have been written purely to test animal trainers. Two hundred animals and sixty trainers headed by Mike Alexander made up the monumental team employed on the set. The starring GSD was played by six different dogs, with Samson as lead. One of the others was a police dog, one was imported from Germany, and two came from Los Angeles rescue groups. Samson was trained by Ray Beal, whom he now lives with, and Jim Dew. He can also be seen briefly in *Hotel for Dogs* (2009).

Chloe is a Chihuahua (played by Angel and voiced by Drew Barrymore) who is used to a pampered, Beverly Hills lifestyle. When Chloe is left in the care of Rachel (Piper Perabo) while her own human (Jamie Lee Curtis) is away, she thinks she has it bad until they go on a trip to Mexico together. Chloe is dognapped and lands in an illegal dogfighting ring, where she is saved by ex-police K-9 Delgado

(Samson, voiced by Andy Garcia). Delgado unwillingly agrees to help Chloe find her way home, never dreaming what danger and difficulties lie in store for them both.

Andy Garcia wanted to meet Samson before beginning to record and was able to spend time with the dog at his house. In the many scenes in which Delgado is seen carrying Chloe in his mouth, he actually carried a coin purse which was replaced in post-production with a CG dog.

Despite poor writing and bad reviews (*People* said the trailer was way more fun than the movie), *Chihuahua* shot up the charts to the number-one movie in America after its opening weekend gross of almost $30 million. Angel was even featured in *Entertainment Weekly* in a lineup of ten new breakout stars in November 2008. The film ended its theatrical run at $92 million, making it one of the most successful dog movies ever.

Beverly Hills Chihuahua 2 (2010)

GSD: *Antonio*

Trainer: Mike Alexander

Director: Alex Zamm

Costar: George Lopez

Country: USA

Status: Availability upcoming

In the summer of 2009, casting director Rich King started the search for dogs to augment the ones provided by Birds & Animals Unlimited for *Beverly Hills Chihuahua 2*. Purebred dogs with unusual talents were sought from around the country to appear in a Beverly Hills canine talent show scene, with live auditions taking place in September. Principle photography for the film began in October 2009 in Los Angeles. Once again, it's not just about Chihuahuas: two of the film's stars are German Shepherd Dogs.

Beverly Hills Chihuahua 2 introduces us to Chloe's new family after she has returned home from her Mexican adventure with Delgado. Her five troublemaking pups take center stage, and two new German Shepherds take over the big-dog role from Delgado: Antonio and Alberto are police dogs in training. A Standard Poodle named Appoline rounds out the A-names.

Although George Lopez returns for the sequel as the voice of Papi, the pups' father, many other cast members are not back for *Beverly Hills Chihuahua 2*. Among the missing are Drew Barrymore, who was Chloe's original voice, and Piper

Perabo as Rachel. Despite criticism from animal welfare groups pertaining to their housing and treatment of exotic animals, Birds & Animals Unlimited continues to take top spots with some of the most demanding animal films ever made. Other new films for the company include the live-action version of the comic strip *Marmaduke* (2010) and *Zookeeper* (2010), about live-action, talking zoo animals and their keeper.

Afterword

In the course of nearly one hundred years and many hundreds of films, the German Shepherd Dog has immortalized itself more thoroughly than any other breed. Anyone who has seen movies has seen a German Shepherd in a movie. To this day, they are saving lives and righting wrongs—or committing the wrongs themselves—in every kind of feature film. They are the epitome of movie dogs, physically and mentally, and have been since the origin of the breed.

Yet to say that the German Shepherd Dog is still the same animal it was with the origin of the breed would be incorrect. The resemblance is faint between the original Rin-Tin-Tin or Peter the Great and Samson or Iago.

In many ways, films themselves have contributed to this drastic change between Max von Stephanitz's German Shepherd Dog and the breed we see today. Without movies, the breed would not have become as popular as quickly as it did in the early twentieth century. Still, the GSDs of movies, from Rin-Tin-Tin to Samson, share two star qualities that universally belong to the breed, whether a hundred years ago or now: intelligence and the desire to work with their humans.

As technology grows, it enhances the safety of canine performers, who are less likely to be placed at risk for a stunt. There are few modern movies with dogs in starring roles where there is not some animatronic or CGI dog work. Concern for the well-being of performing animals has grown with public awareness and will hopefully continue to increase in the years to come. However, there are still many movies which slip through the cracks.

Employing the American Humane Association's on-set supervision unfortunately comes at the expense of the film's producers and is often skipped as a result. *It is not required by law for any animal welfare representative of any kind to monitor how animals are treated on film sets in any country in the world.*

The AHA sometimes raises awareness about films which have mistreated animals, such as the 2001 French film *Brotherhood of the Wolf*, which employed horses, a wolf, a large group of shy Saarloos Wolfdogs, and many others. But it does so selectively. There are a great number of recent films which abused animals, such as *Kazan*, which the AHA not only did not supervise—despite the film being produced within their area of jurisdiction—but also made no protest against. When contacted for the purposes of this book, the AHA declined to discuss any of the films it was asked about.

Yet for the most part, the quality of working conditions for film animals has increased over the years and will hopefully continue to improve with the aid of public awareness.

There are hundreds more films starring German Shepherd Dogs that this book does not cover. If you were unable to find your own favorite GSD movie listed here, or are interested in more titles, please visit www.reeldogspress.com, where the author keeps a frequently updated list of over four hundred German Shepherd movies. If you have new information about a film or dog mentioned in these pages, please contact the author, also through the above website.

As we move into a new decade, we can look forward to more German Shepherd Dog films and more canine heroes—and, it can be hoped, more heroes in the category of trainers. Often uncredited and overlooked, a great trainer can mean the difference between not only a jaw-dropping performance versus an uninspired one, but an animal who is in love with his or her work, rather than stressed or frightened.

The trainers who have done more for German Shepherd Dogs in film over the past nine decades than any others include five men and one woman who largely made the breed's film legacy possible. So to Lee Duncan, Earl Johnson, Frank Barnes, Dorothy Crider, Charles Eisenmann, and Karl Lewis Miller, thank you. We look forward to another nine decades of German Shepherd Dogs through your successors and the successors of your Wonder Dogs.

Acknowledgments

Heartfelt thanks to Leigh Allen Taylor, without whom this book would not only not have been written but would not have seen the light of day once it had. Thanks also to Matt Levine. And to Matt Feisthammel for getting the words in place.

A huge thank you to Tony and Katie Nikl for your generosity with your time and for sharing your stories and your dogs with me. You make this business worth writing about. Also to Barbara Kelso—though I was a stranger, you could not have been more gracious. Thanks for all of your assistance to Les Adams, Rob Bloch, Barbara Kolk, Helmut Lüking, and Sandy Moore. And to Siw Ågren of Animal Rights Sweden, Odd Harald Eidsmo of Dyrebeskyttelsen Norge, Anton Krag of the Norwegian Animal Protection Alliance, and Ingrid Rudefors of the Stockholm Film Commission.

Thank you, Daphne Hereford, for your help with photographs and for keeping the legacy of Rin-Tin-Tin alive. Thanks to Stephanie Ogle for finding so many resources for me and always being willing to hunt for more.

Thanks also to you, the readers and viewers, who love dogs and movies.

Merchants

The top websites for locating most of the films profiled in this book are:

www.amazon.com (often through dealers of used videos)

www.ebay.com

www.grapevinevideo.com

www.nostalgiafamilyvideo.com

www.moviesunlimted.com

www.lifeisamovie.com

Sources

Ackerley, J. R. *We Think the World of You*. New York: Poseidon Press, 1989.

Alwyn, Cynthia G. *Scent of Murder*. New York: St. Martin's Minotaur, 2001.

Badley, Linda. Palmer, R. Barton. Schneider, Steven Jay (editors). *Traditions in World Cinema*. Piscataway, NJ: Rutgers University Press, 2006.

Bartel, Pauline. *Amazing Animal Actors*. Dallas, TX: Taylor Publishing Company, 1997.

Basinger, Jeanine. *Silent Stars*. Darby, PA: Diane Publishing Co., 1999.

Beebe, Lloyd. *Wilderness Trails and a Dream: The Story Behind the Olympic Game Farm*. Sequim, WA, 1995.

Beck, Ken. Clark, Jim. *The Encyclopedia of TV Pets*. Nashville, TN: Rutledge Hill Press, 2002.

Blyton, Enid. *Five Go Off to Camp*. London, England: Hobber & Stoughton Ltd., 1980.

Blyton, Enid. *Five Have a Mystery to Solve*. London, England: Hobber & Stoughton Ltd., 1980.

Brockwell, David. *The Police Dog*. New York: G. Howard Watt, 1925.

Burnam, John C., MSgt (U.S.A. Ret.). *A Soldier's Best Friend: Scout Dogs and Their Handlers in the Vietnam War*. New York: Basic Books, 2003.

Burt, Jonathan. *Animals in Film*. London, England: Reaktion Books, 2003.

Corbin, William. *Smoke*. New York: Coward-McCann, 1967.

Curwood, James Oliver. *Baree, Son of Kazan*. New York: Grosset & Dunlap, 1917.

Curwood, James Oliver. *Kazan, the Wolf Dog*. New York: Grosset & Dunlap, 1941.

Eames, John Douglas. *The MGM Story*. New York: Crown Publishing, Inc., 1975.

Edelson, Edward. *Great Animals of the Movies*. New York: Doubleday, 1980.

Eisenmann, Charles P. *Stop! Sit! and Think*. East Syracuse, NY: MacDonald-Redmore, Inc., 1968.

Eisenmann, Charles P. *A Dog's Day in Court*. Toronto, Canada: The Bryant Press Ltd., 1983.

Evarts, Hal G. *The Cross Pull*. New York: Alfred A. Knopf, 1920.

Fienup-Riordan, Ann. *Freeze Frame: Alaskan Eskimos in the Movies*. Seattle, WA: University of Washington Press, 2003.

Fisher, David. *The Long Dark Night*. New York: Ballantine Books, 1977.

Fogle, Bruce, D.V.M. *The Encyclopedia of the Dog*. New York: Dorling Kindersley Publishing, Inc., 1995.

Foglesong, Clara. *Peter: The Real Story of a "Reel" Dog*. Harvard Press, 1945.

Gary, Romain. *White Dog*. New York: The New American Library Company, Inc., 1970.

Goldrup, Jim. Goldrup, Tom. *Growing Up on the Set: Interviews with 39 Former Child Actors of Classic Film and Television*. Jefferson, NC: McFarland & Company, 2002.

Grant, Reg. *World War II: The Events and Their Impact on Real People*. New York: Dorling Kindersley Publishing, Inc., 2008.

Grossman, Loyd. *The Dog's Tale: A History of Man's Best Friend*. London, England: BBC Books, 1993.

Hall, Becky. *Morris and Buddy: The Story of the First Seeing Eye Dog*. Morton Grove, Illinois: Albert Whitman & Company, 2007.

Hamlyn, Paul. *Dogs, Dogs, Dogs, Dogs*. Feltham, Middlesex, England: The Hamlyn Publishing Group Ltd., 1968.

Heston, Charlton. *In the Arena: An Autobiography*. New York: Boulevard Books, 1997.

Holman, Arthur. *Dog Versus Crime*. London, England: Pan Books Ltd., 1959.

Kammerer, Roger. *Recollections of Pitt County*. Charleston, SC: History Press, 2006.

Kendrick, Baynard. *The Odor of Violets*. Philadelphia, PA: Triangle Books, 1945.

Koehler, William R. *The Koehler Method of Dog Training*. New York: Howell Book House, Inc., 1981.

Koehler, William R. *The Wonderful World of Disney Animals*. New York: Howell Book House, Inc., 1979.

Sources

Lee, Raymond. *Not So Dumb: The Life and Times of Animal Actors*. New York: Castle Books, 1970.

London, Jack. *The Call of the Wild*. New York: Grosset & Dunlap, 1983.

London, Jack. *White Fang*. New York: Anness Publishing, Ltd., 1996.

London, Jack. *That Spot*. New York: Grosset & Dunlap, 1983.

Malcolmson, David. *London; the Dog Who Made the Team*. New York: Duell, Sloan and Pearce, 1963.

Maltin, Leonard. *The Disney Films*. New York: Crown Publishing, Inc., 1973.

Matheson, Richard. *I Am Legend*. New York: Tom Doherty Associates, LLC, 2007.

Morey, Walt. *Kavik the Wolf Dog*. New York: E.P. Dutton, 1968.

Orr, Gertrude. *Dog Stars of Hollywood*. Akron, OH: The Saalfield Publishing Company, 1936.

Shields, Allan. *The Spirit of Rin-Tin-Tin*. Clovis, CA, 2001.

Silverman, Stephen M. *Movie Mutts: Hollywood Goes to the Dogs*. New York: Harry N. Abrams, Inc., 2001.

Smith, Wayne. *Thor*. New York: St. Martin's Press, 1992.

Trimble, Lawrence. *Strongheart: The Story of a Wonder Dog*. Racine, WI: Whitman Publishing Company, 1926.

Tuska, Jon. *The Vanishing Legion: A History of Mascot Pictures, 1927–1935*. Jefferson, NC: McFarland & Company, Inc., 1999.

Warner Brothers Productions. *The Story of Rin-Tin-Tin: The Marvelous & Amazing Dog of the Movies*. Racine, WI: Whitman Publishing Company, 1927.

Other Print Publications

Boys' Cinema Weekly. Vol. 10. No. 246., Aug 23, 1924.

Classic Combined with Shadowland. Vol. 18. No. 3., November 1923

Entreatment Weekly. No. 1021/1022., Nov 21, 2008

Entreatment Weekly. No. 1016., Oct 17, 2008

The New York Times, various articles from historical *New York Times* archives.

People. Vol. 70. No. 26., Dec 29, 2008

People. Vol. 70. No. 15., Oct 13, 2008

The San Rafael / Terra Linda News Pointer. Feb 5-11, 1992. Article by Win Murphy.

Starburst. Issue 358, Vol. 33. No. 12., Jan 2008

Pressbooks

Bad Moon. Warner Brothers Pictures, 1996.

Big Cat, The. Eagle-Lion Films, 1949.

Courage of the North. Stage & Screen Productions, 1935.

Dog's Best Friend, A. United Artists, 1960.

Fangs of the Arctic. Allied Artists Pictures, 1953.

Littlest Hobo, The. Allied Artists Pictures, 1958.

My Dog Shep. Screen Guild Productions, 1946.

Rusty Leads the Way. Columbia Pictures Corporation, 1948.

Silent Witness. Monogram Pictures, 1943.

We Think the World of You. Cinecom Pictures, 1988.

When Lightning Strikes. Regal Productions, 1934.

Wolf Call. Monogram Pictures, 1939.

Wolf Dog. Twentieth Century Fox Film Corporation, 1958.

Won Ton Ton, the Dog Who Saved Hollywood. Paramount Pictures, 1976.

Electronic Sources

AllMovie
> http://www.allmovie.com/

American Humane Association Movie Ratings
> http://www.ahafilm.info/movies/ratings.phtml

Animals of Montana
> http://www.animalsofmontana.com/

Beyond Just Bears
> http://www.creativeanimaltalent.com/

Books Into Films
> http://booksintofilms.com/

Boone's Animals for Hollywood
> http://www.boonesanimals.com/

British Film Institute
> http://www.bfi.org.uk/

Bruffmore Kennels, Inc.
> http://www.bruffmore.com/

Bugga C's German Shepherd Site
> http://home.comcast.net/~buggartt/newpage2.html

Sources

Canczech Dogs
    http://www.canczechdogs.com/
The CBS Children's Film Festival with Kukla, Fran and Ollie
    http://kukla.tv/cbs.html
chron.com
    http://www.chron.com/
City of Shreveport
    http://www.ci.shreveport.la.us/
The Clara Bow Filmography Page
    http://theclarabowpage.tripod.com/blacklightning.html
Club Español del Berger Blanc Suisse
    http://www.cebbs.es/
Critters of the Cinema
    http://www.crittersofthecinema.com/
Cyriac Family History Project
    http://hollywood.fred.cyriac-fhp.com/
Dogs in the News
    http://dogsinthenews.com/
Entertainment Weekly
    http://www.ew.com/
EzineArticles
    http://ezinearticles.com/
Fandango
    http://www.fandango.com/
Fantastic Fiction
    http://www.fantasticfiction.co.uk/
Film in America
    http://www.filminamerica.com/
Georgia K9 Academy
    http://gak9.com/
GSD League Working Branch
    http://www.gsdleague-workingbranch.com/index.html
Guide Dogs for the Blind
    http://www.guidedogs.com/
Haaretz Daily Newspaper Israel
    http://www.haaretz.com/

HebrewOnline Newsletter
   http://www.hebrewonline.com/Newsletters/dogs_2008.asp
HighBeam Research
   http://www.highbeam.com/
Hong Kong Film Archive
   http://www.lcsd.gov.hk/CE/CulturalService/HKFA/en/index.php
International White Shepherd Library
   http://www.whiteshepherd.info/
Internet Movie Database
   http://www.imdb.com/
Israeli Films
   http://www.israelifilms.co.il/
Kung Fu Cinema
   http://www.kungfucinema.com/
La Scuola dei Campioni S.r.l.
   http://www.lascuoladeicampioni.it/
Lary Mak
   http://www.larymak.com/
Los Angeles Times
   http://www.latimes.com/
Military.com
   http://www.military.com/
Moviehole
   http://www.moviehole.net/
Pedigree Database
   http://www.pedigreedatabase.com/
Rich King Casting
   http://www.richkingcasting.net/
The Seeing Eye
   http://www.seeingeye.org/
Shreveport K-9 Search and Rescue
   http://www.shreveportla.gov/dept/fire/one/aboutUs.htm
The Spaghetti Western Database
   http://www.spaghetti-western.net/
Steve Berens' Animals of Distinction
   http://www.berensanimals.com/

Sources

Stirling County Schutzhund Club
    http://www.stirlingcountyschutzhundclub.co.uk/
Topix
    http://www.topix.com/
Turner Classic Movies
    http://www.tcm.com/
Uncle Moshe's Farm
    http://www.dodmoshe.com/
Variety
    http://www.variety.com/
Weatherwax Dogs and the Movies
    http://home.att.net/~weatherwax/
White German Shepherd Dog Club of America, Inc.
    http://www.wgsdca.org/
Wikipedia
    http://wikipedia.org/
Wolfdog.org
    http://www.wolfdog.org/eng/
The Writing Studio
    http://www.writingstudio.co.za/
WUSV 2007
    http://wusv2007.tripod.com/
Your Video Store Shelf
    http://yourvideostoreshelf.com/
Zwitserse Witte Herder Kennel vd Renessehoeve
    http://www.vdrenessehoeve.nl/

Miscellaneous

America First flyer, circa 1928.

Harold from *Under the Black Eagle*. Metro-Goldwyn-Mayer, 1928.

Investment proposal book from *Rin Tin Tin*, compiled by Herbert Leonard, 1996.

NPR's *All Things Considered*, Oct 7, 2008.

Original script from *The Pack*, written by Robert Clouse. Warner Brothers Pictures, 1977.

Index of Dogs

Index

Index of Humans

Index

Index

Index

Index of Movies

Index

Index

General Index

Index

Index

Index

About the Author

Jordan Taylor is an avid reader and writer of both fiction and nonfiction. As a professional dog trainer, she provides dogs for film and print media. Jordan is a movie dog expert with over four hundred pieces of canine film memorabilia and over seven hundred dog movies in her personal collection. She writes a blog about historical and contemporary movie canines.

Jordan writes and lives with two dogs in the Pacific Northwest.

www.reeldogspress.com
reeldogs.blogspot.com